032

£5

proof of the pudding

proof of the

pudding

PHIL VICKERY

PHOTOGRAPHS BY STEVE BAXTER

SIMON & SCHUSTER

A VIACOM COMPANY

First published in Great Britain by Simon & Schuster UK Ltd, 2003

A Viacom Company

Paperback edition, 2004

Copyright © Phil Vickery, 2003

Simon & Schuster UK Ltd

Africa House

64–78 Kingsway

London

WC2B 6AH

This book is copyright under the Berne Convention.

No reproduction without permission.

All rights reserved.

The right of to be identified as the Authors of this Work has been
asserted by them in accordance with sections 77 and 78 of the
Copyright, Designs and Patents Act, 1988.

1 3 5 7 9 10 8 6 4 2

Managing Editor: Susanna Clarke

Design: Jane Humphrey

Home economist for photography: Linda Tubby

Stylist for photography: Liz Belton

Copy editor: Deborah Savage

Typesetting: Stylize Digital Artwork

Printed and bound in China

ISBN 0 74322 053 6 hardback

ISBN 0 74322 054 4 paperback

Puddings are my personal passion.

I want to take the fear out of puddings and to show why

puddings are so wonderful to cook, and to eat. PHIL VICKERY

FOR MY MUM

There are a few people I'd like to thank,
because without their help this book would not have been possible.

Firstly, Sam Boyce, who set the whole thing up and like me, thank goodness,
believed that great British puddings are the best in the world.

My mother, not only for cooking some of the best puddings and cakes in the land,
but also for putting up with all the mess when I was at college.

My father because I left him out of the last book and he has never let me
forget it, and for introducing me at an early age to the great combination of
golden syrup on spotted dick and skin on custard.

Brian Gilham, by far the best 'old school' pastry chef in the land.

Julia Algar, not only for agreeing to re-cook and edit every recipe and doing a
fantastic job, but also for making my food look good on telly for the past 6 years.

Billington's sugar for making the job easy and a real pleasure.

Susanna Clarke at Simon & Schuster for being very supportive
and understanding.

And last, but definitely not least, Fernie, for struggling through doughnut week,
Christmas cake week, pastry week, ice cream week etc., etc., over the past 2 $^1/_2$ years.
And for simply being the best wife any man could wish for.

CONTENTS

introduction

The proof of the pudding is what the British have been missing out on for the last twenty years. Hasn't eating desserts, let alone preparing them, become for many people almost a lost art? Yet for centuries Britain invented, cooked and consumed in vast quantities superb puddings, cakes, breads, confections, ice creams, fools and syllabubs. They range from famous names such as Bakewell Tart or Saffron Walden cake, through old-fashioned staples like Lancashire parkin, to the forgotten glories of London syllabub and Eton mess. The titles of these desserts conjure up their own world; some of them are even staples of everyday speech – think of the much-mocked spotted dick and custard. Everybody has heard of it, but how many of us these days really know how delicious it can be and why it was always such a favourite?

The Europeans have taken care to preserve their traditional pastry cooking and confectionery. France is rightly famous for its pies, breads and tarts. You only need to amble down any – and I mean any – French street and you will find the local patisserie window shelves groaning with *tarte au citron*, croissant, *pain au chocolat*, brioche, strawberry tarts and madeleines. Italy prides itself on its sweet cookery: *biscotti*, *pannacotta* and, my favourite, *panettone*. Apple strudel is a classic not only of Austria but also the Balkans and Hungary. We readily buy Danish pastries; of course I love them all. Belgian waffles are by far the best, as are their chocolates. I've eaten plenty of both in the small cafés and bars around the Grand Place in Brussels. In Greece and Turkey they consume huge amounts of sweet things – baklava and halva to name just two. The Greeks even shower newly-weds with sugared almonds.

But while it has been fashionable to celebrate continental specialities, it sometimes seems we know more about these than our own home-grown triumphs. These days most British restaurants, hotels, bars and bistros confine their dessert range to about ten puddings – typically crème brulée, chocolate fondant, tiramisu, sticky toffee pudding, apple pie, chocolate tart, and so on. While all of these are potentially great desserts, the pudding course does seem to have become something of an afterthought, and a rather sad one at that.

The truth is that our islands actually produce a vast number of unique fruits and nuts which are prized by the dedicated pastry chef. Our greengages, for example, are as good as the French mirabelles. Our West Country cream and apples, Yorkshire forced rhubarb, Scottish raspberries, Kent cob and hazel nuts, Lancashire whimberries – these are what make the British pastry chef's work entirely distinctive. Our mulberries are simply the tastiest fruits in the world, so good in fact that the nursery rhyme must once have evoked all the tastes of summer on that cold and frosty morning.

MILK & CREAM
PUDDINGS

Milk and cream puddings
are the most comforting and
satisfying in the world,
conjuring up memories of
Sunday lunch on cold, rainy
days, or teatime after a day out
in the snow. When I was a
child my family would fight so
much over who got the skin
off the rice pudding or custard
that my dad would have to
divide it into tiny portions so
that everyone could have a
share!

The British love affair with
hot, milky puddings began
back in medieval times, when
large amounts of almonds were
crushed and mixed with milk
and honey to make the first
milk puddings. Almonds were
imported from Italy, where
they formed the basis for a
crude type of blancmange –
and, of course, vast quantities

of marzipan. They also became popular as a valuable source of protein during Lent, when meat was forbidden. They found their way into all manner of savoury dishes as a replacement for chicken and pork.

The quintessential rice pudding came into its own in Victorian times, either boiled or baked, with dried fruits in winter and fresh fruit in summer. There were all sorts of other flavourings too: the Victorians particularly liked folding in marigold petals, giving the finished pudding a vibrant colour. Spices such as cinnamon and nutmeg were all the rage, and the ultimate fashion accessory for Victorian gentlemen was an ornate silver nutmeg box, so that they could have a whole nutmeg on their person at all times, for grating on to their drinks and puddings. Mrs Beeton suggests a variation 'suitable for a winter pudding when fresh fruits are not available' involving flavouring your baked sweet rice pudding with beef marrow, brandy, nutmeg and lemon, and baking it in a pastry case. She says that 'slices of candied peel may be added at pleasure'.

In fact, cold, baked or boiled rice pudding can be changed dramatically by the addition of candied lemon, lime or even quinces, along with crème fraîche or double cream. Fresh vanilla also works well, as does Yorkshire forced rhubarb and syrup.

Ground and flaked rice are far less popular than they used to be, but both are wonderful. I loved a brand called Creamola rice as a child, hot with jam, and also a pudding made with flaked rice (which is basically a flattened rice grain), cooked and then mixed with summer blueberries and cream. Queen of Puddings is one of my all-time favourites, a classic combination of cake crumbs (best of all Madeira cake), hot milk, meringue, and raspberry and greengage jams.

This chapter is dedicated to real comfort food, and just shows what can be done with the humble grain of rice, piece of cake and pint of milk when you put your mind to it.

see also

custard brioches *page 77*

deep-fried custard with honey and lemon
    page 78

chocolate bread and butter pudding
    page 93

hot and cold chocolate milk shake with
    cookies *page 94*

caramel macaroni meringue pudding
    page 138

eton mess with rose-petal sauce *page 227*

rice pudding
with rose-hip syrup and crème fraîche

for the rose-hip syrup
350 g (12 oz) soft rose-hips
400 g (14 oz) granulated sugar
juice of 1 lemon

for the rice pudding
600 ml (1 pint) whole milk
1 vanilla pod, split
55 g (2 oz) short-grain rice
175 g (6 oz) crème fraîche
juice of 1 lime, to serve

serves 4

Rose-hips are the fruit of the wild dog rose. They were served in the Middle Ages as a sweet – how they cooked them I do not know – but they do make a very good syrup.

The best time to pick rose-hips is late October, early November when they are starting to soften after the first frost, similar to rowan berries. Any earlier and they are too hard and have not developed their unique flavour. Do not leave it too late, though, or the birds will get there before you. Rose-hips freeze well.

To make the rose-hip syrup, wash the rose-hips well and remove any stalks or calyxes. Process in a food processor until you have a thick purée.

Bring 500 ml (18 fl oz) of water to the boil in a pan, add the purée and then bring back to the boil and simmer for 2 minutes. Remove from the heat and leave to stand for a further 20 minutes. Strain the mixture through a piece of muslin or clean tea towel, reserving both the juice and pulp.

Bring another 500 ml (18 fl oz) of water to the boil and add the reserved pulp. Simmer for 2 minutes, then strain again.

Mix the two strained juices together and simmer rapidly in a pan to reduce until you have about 1 litre (1¾ pints). Add the sugar and lemon juice and stir until dissolved. Simmer rapidly until the syrup is deeply coloured and has reduced to about 400 ml (14 fl oz). Strain and then allow to cool. Pour the syrup into a clean jar or bottle and keep in the fridge (this will keep in the fridge for about 3 weeks).

To make the rice pudding, preheat the oven to 180°C/350°F/Gas Mark 4. Pour the milk into an ovenproof pan, scrape in the vanilla seeds, add the vanilla pod and bring to the boil. Sprinkle in the rice, stir, then cover with a lid, transfer to the oven and bake for about 45 minutes, or until thick and creamy.

Remove from the oven and stir well, then replace the lid and allow to cool for 20 minutes. After this time stir in the crème fraîche and enough rose-hip syrup to flavour the rice. Serve hot or cold, with an additional drizzle of syrup and a squeeze of fresh lime juice over the top.

rice pudding
with dried bananas and brown sugar

410 g can of evaporated milk

about 200 ml (7 fl oz) whole milk

1 vanilla pod, split

55 g (2 oz) short-grain rice

soft brown sugar, to taste

125 g (4½ oz) dried bananas, chopped

175 g (6 oz) crème fraîche

serves 4

This is very different from the recipe opposite. Here I almost marinate the dried bananas in the pudding and this, along with the evaporated milk, gives it a very caramelly edge.

Just recently, rice pudding has become trendy again. Gone are the days of the thick sludge that we were forced to eat at school; nowadays, it can be eaten hot, cold in a mousse or even as a soufflé as my old pal Paul Kitching does at his Juniper restaurant in Altrincham, which is gorgeous. Flavourings vary from cinnamon, prunes, nutmeg, bananas and stewed apples in the hot version, to clotted cream, crème fraîche, rose- and orange-flower waters, basil, and butterscotch in chilled rice puddings. Either way, rice pudding is a real favourite of mine. The addition of evaporated milk and crème fraîche gives the pudding a really rich twist.

Forget about the calories just this once and enjoy yourself!

Preheat the oven to 180°C/350°F/Gas Mark 4. Pour the evaporated milk into a measuring jug. Top up with the milk until you have 600 ml (1 pint). Pour into an ovenproof, preferably non-stick, thick-bottomed saucepan, add the vanilla pod and bring to the boil very slowly – stir all the time or it will burn.

Once the milk is boiling, rain in the rice and stir well. Cover with a tightly fitting lid, transfer to the oven and bake for about 1 hour, stirring every 10–15 minutes. If the rice becomes too thick or dry during cooking you can add an extra splash of milk.

When the rice is tender, remove from the oven and stir well. Take out the vanilla pod and add brown sugar to taste, it's up to you how sweet you want the whole thing. Leave to cool for about 5 minutes.

Stir in the chopped dried bananas and crème fraîche and leave again for a few minutes for the bananas to soften; then serve. I think that rice pudding that is too hot is awful, you can't taste it or even eat it, so do leave it to stand for a while before you tuck in.

chilled creamed rice
with candied pineapple

600 ml (1 pint) whole milk

1 vanilla pod, split

55 g (2 oz) pudding rice

100 ml (3½ fl oz) double cream

200 g (7 oz) crème fraîche

heaped 60 ml (4 tablespoons)
unrefined icing sugar

finely grated zest and juice of 1 large lemon

100 g (3½ oz) candied or semi-dried
pineapple, cut into very small cubes

30 ml (2 tablespoons) chopped fresh mint

My Mum's Shortbread (page 298), to serve

serves 4

Chilled creamed rice with pineapple is not a new idea, but it is delicious. You can set the pudding with gelatine, but I tend to like the cooked rice just on its own.

On a recent trip to Florence I happened to pop into the central market and found the most wonderful selection of soft, candied fruits. Everything from baby plums to strawberries and even tomatoes were for sale. Candied fruits can be bought all year round now in Britain, and there are some very good ones too: melon, figs and plums can all be bought fairly easily. A little goes a long way so don't go mad.

Preheat the oven to 150°C/300°F/Gas Mark 2.

Bring the milk and vanilla pod to the boil in an ovenproof pan. Rain in the rice and stir well, then cover with a tightly fitting lid, place in the oven and cook for 35–40 minutes, or until thick and creamy. Remove from the oven and allow to cool.

When cool, spoon into a large bowl and break up with a wooden spoon. Add the cream, crème fraîche, icing sugar and lemon zest and juice and mix well. Finally, add the pineapple and mint and fold in together. Chill well, preferably overnight.

Serve in deep bowls, with shortbread.

gooseberry and elderflower fool
with crushed meringues

225 g (8 oz) gooseberries, topped and tailed

2 egg whites (optional)

600 ml (1 pint) double cream, softly whipped

about 30–45 ml (2–3 tablespoons)
elderflower cordial

2 individual meringues, or meringue nests,
crushed into small pieces

castor sugar, to taste

serves 4

Every year in early summer I used to walk my dog, Max, past some wonderful elderberry trees and each time I thought about the delicious syrup you can make from the elderflowers.

Some chefs deep-fry the flowers to serve with ice cream but I think they are vile. There really are only three ways to use these delicate flowers – syrup, added to gooseberries when bottling, and in 'elderflower champagne', now called 'sparkling elderflower apéritif' since the French got funny about the use of the name champagne.

If you are lucky enough to have a nearby tree you can gather the flowers and make your own cordial; if not, you can buy elderflower cordial now, so why not invest in a bottle and try this sweet – it's simple, very tasty and one of my favourites!

For caramel-flavoured meringues, which are great in this recipe, try Microwave Meringues (page 132), using unrefined golden icing sugar.

This recipe contains raw or lightly cooked eggs. Because of the slight risk of salmonella poisoning, these should be avoided by the sick, the elderly, the very young, and pregnant women.

Place the gooseberries in a pan with 50 ml (2 fl oz) of water and bring to a simmer. Reduce the heat and cook gently for about 15–20 minutes, or until the gooseberries have turned to a thick, chunky purée. Remove from the heat and allow to cool.

If using, whisk the egg whites until they form soft peaks; do not over whisk them (see page 129).

Place the gooseberry purée in a bowl, add the whipped cream and fold in, and then add elderflower cordial to taste. Finally, fold in the egg whites if using, and crushed meringues. If necessary, add castor sugar to sweeten to taste.

Spoon the fool into glasses and serve straight away.

Yorkshire rhubarb fool
in a mug

600 g (1 lb 5 oz) new-season rhubarb, cut
into 2.5 cm (1-inch) pieces

85 g (3 oz) unrefined castor sugar

juice of 1 large lemon

1 vanilla pod, split

about 48 sponge fingers
(about 275 g/9½ oz)

300 ml (½ pint) whipping cream,
whipped to soft peaks

450 ml (16 fl oz) thick custard (good-quality
ready-made custard is quite good for this)

for the sauce

225 g (8 oz) new-season rhubarb, chopped

100 g (3½ oz) castor sugar

lemon juice

serves 6

A third of the world's supply of new-season (forced) rhubarb is grown in Yorkshire and it makes a delicate and delicious fool. This is a different way of serving fool from the usual wine glasses and I rather like it. Using Savoy sponge fingers adds a little texture.

Gently cook the rhubarb in a pan with the sugar, lemon juice and vanilla pod for about 4–5 minutes, or until the rhubarb is softened, thick and pulpy. Cool completely and then remove the vanilla pod.

The rest is relatively easy! Line six large, straight-sided tea mugs, about 8 cm (3 inches) in diameter and 300 ml (½ pint) capacity, with cling film – if you wet the inside of the mugs first it's a lot easier. Then line the sides with sponge fingers.

Carefully fold together the whipped cream, custard and cooled rhubarb. Use the mixture to fill up the mugs, tap down to level and then cover with cling film and chill well (overnight is best if possible).

To make the sauce, gently stew the rhubarb with the sugar and 100 ml (3½ fl oz) of water until soft and stringy. Carefully liquidise and pass through a fine sieve. Add a squeeze of lemon juice and taste; you may need to add more sugar if the sauce is too sour.

Turn out by gently pulling the cling film – the fools will slide out. Serve with a little rhubarb sauce.

bramley apple, caramel
and custard fool

2 Bramley apples, peeled, cored and chopped
into 1 cm (½-inch) pieces
finely grated zest and juice of 1 lemon
250 g (9 oz) granulated sugar
450 ml (16 fl oz) custard (make your own, or
use a good-quality brand such as Bird's)
600 ml (1 pint) very cold whipping cream,
lightly whipped

serves 4

Bramleys are really cheap and great value for money at any time of year. Their unique tartness combined with the dark caramel and custard makes this fool a delicious, light ending to a meal. The secrets are not to add sugar to the stewed apples, to use whipping cream rather than double, its heavier brother, for a light, tasty treat, and to use wine glasses so you can see the layers of great colours

To make the 'apple marmalade', heat the prepared apple in a pan with the lemon zest and juice and cook gently for about 10 minutes, or until the apple is tender – you may need to add a touch of water as the apple cooks if it starts to thicken too much. Once cooked, allow to cool (don't worry too much if there are a few undercooked lumps).

Meanwhile, place the sugar in a pan and just cover with water. Bring to the boil and then boil rapidly until the syrup starts to thicken and get darker – keep a careful eye on it as it can burn very quickly indeed (see page 171).

When the caramel is dark brown, carefully tip in 150 ml (¼ pint) of cold water – there will be a lot of spluttering and splashing, so stand back and don't worry about that. Bring the syrup back to the boil and allow any pieces of caramel to melt. Pour into a bowl or jug and leave to cool completely.

To serve, place a little of the apple marmalade in the bottom of four large wine glasses and then pour on some of the caramel syrup. Next, add a spoonful of custard and finally a spoonful of cream. Repeat to fill the glasses. Chill for 15 minutes before serving with shortbread or just on its own with a cup of strong coffee.

crème brûlée

6 large egg yolks

55 g (2 oz) castor sugar

600 ml (1 pint) whipping cream

zest of 1 large lemon, taken off with a peeler

1 vanilla pod, split

There are three recipes that I had always vowed I'd never put into a pudding book: chocolate fondant, tiramisù, and crème brûlée. The reason being that, for the past six or seven years, all you have seen on dessert menus have been these three puddings plus a sprinkling of others and, generally speaking, all are pretty poor relations of the real things. However, after a long think I realise no pudding book could be without crème brûlée (the jury's still out on the other two!).

Every chef seems to have a twist on crème brûlée and there have been some real disasters! Please listen to me, there is, and will only ever be one crème brûlée, made with just egg, cream, sugar, vanilla and a touch of lemon oil from the zest.

The three most common problems with crème brûlée are:

1 Overcooked or unevenly cooked custard, mostly due to incorrect oven temperature;

2 Using too much egg, so it ends up like an ice hockey puck; and

3 Using double cream, which makes the finished crème brûlée heavy.

Oh and by the way, this is another classic example of the French stealing a great British idea, giving it a sexy name and calling it their own.

Preheat the oven to 140°C/275°F/Gas Mark 1. Place the egg yolks and castor sugar in a bowl and gently mix together.

Place the cream, lemon zest and vanilla pod in a pan and slowly bring to the boil. Once boiling, pour on to the beaten egg yolks and sugar, whisk together well and then leave to cool and infuse for 10 minutes.

Strain the mixture through a sieve then pour into four 9.5 cm diameter × 5 cm deep (4- × 2-inch) ramekins. (There has been a trend recently to cook brûlées in very shallow dishes. This is also not right in my eyes: the cooked custard should be dense, deep and just a bit wobbly in the middle.) Carefully place in a deep baking tray, and pour boiling water from a kettle into the tray until the water is halfway up the side of the ramekins. Cover the whole tray lightly with foil and bake for 30 minutes, or until just set. Remember the residual heat in the custard will carry on the cooking process for a good 10 minutes or so once out of the oven. Remove from the oven and leave to cool, then chill well, preferably overnight.

When you come to glaze the brûlée, sprinkle a thin layer of castor sugar on top of each, taking care to make sure all the custard is covered. Place under a very hot grill, or (far better) glaze nice and evenly with a blowtorch, and then cool slightly. Repeat the process and then leave to harden before serving (see page 39). I like to glaze the brûlée just before the start of the meal, then they have time to warm up slightly. There is nothing worse than ice-cold crème brûlée!

almond blancmange
with rose-petal syrup

250 g (9 oz) unblanched almonds

600 ml (1 pint) whole milk

125 g (4½ oz) castor sugar

6 egg yolks

4½ gelatine leaves, soaked in cold water
(see page 99)

200 ml (7 fl oz) whipping cream,
lightly whipped

Rose-Petal Syrup (page 234) to serve

serves 4

Forget any thoughts of school blancmange, that face-pack-pink, rubbery, tasteless pap we were forced to eat. This is real blancmange: light, creamy and delicious with rose-petal or saffron syrup, a crumbly shortbread biscuit and some sweet English strawberries or raspberries at room temperature.

The whole idea of a blancmange is that the texture should be light and creamy but not too rich, and it must have the essential 'wobble' factor when the plate is moved from side to side. This dessert was part of the meal that won me Chef of the Year a few years ago.

Place the almonds in a food processor and blitz until you have a crumbly powder; alternatively, crush them with a rolling pin. Place in a large heatproof bowl.

Boil the milk and pour on to the almonds, cover and leave to infuse for at least 2 hours (it's really best left overnight).

After this time, strain the almonds from the milk, pushing all the milk out with the back of a ladle or large spoon. Measure the milk, and top it back up to 600 ml (1 pint) with fresh milk if necessary – this is very important or the finished blancmange will set too firmly. Discard the almonds.

Place the sugar and egg yolks in a bowl and whisk for about 5 minutes or until light and creamy. Bring the almond milk to the boil and pour on to the sugar and egg mixture; whisk together and return to the pan. Cook over a very low heat, stirring all the time until lightly thickened, but do not overcook – if the mixture thickens too much and looks as though it is starting to separate, pour it into a liquidiser, or use a hand-blender and blitz for a couple of seconds: the mixture will be slightly thinner but still usable. Pass through a fine strainer into a clean bowl.

Next, gently squeeze excess water out of the soaked gelatine, add to the hot custard and stir well until dissolved. Sit the bowl in a large bowl of iced water and stir constantly until the mixture is cool and starting to thicken. Lightly fold the cream into the cooled mixture fairly quickly using a whisk; then pour into 150 ml (¼-pint) ramekins, glasses or bowls. Chill until set, for at least 2 hours, before serving with rose-petal syrup.

Fern's queen of puddings

600 ml (1 pint) whole milk

1 vanilla pod, split

3 large eggs, separated

25 g (1 oz) castor sugar

85 g (3 oz) Madeira cake crumbs
or fine breadcrumbs

a pinch of freshly grated nutmeg

finely grated zest of 1 lemon

for the topping

a pinch of cream of tartar

85 g (3 oz) castor sugar, plus
extra to decorate

85 g (3 oz) icing sugar, sifted

about 45 ml (3 tablespoons) greengage or
green rhubarb jam

about 45 ml (3 tablespoons) raspberry jam

serves 4–6

One of Fern's favourite puddings. Making this as apprentices, we would always finish the top with greengage and raspberry jams: the contrasting colours are essential (Tiptree make a very good greengage jam). The secret is to not overcook the custard. Any cake or breadcrumbs will do but I just love buttery Madeira cake. This and egg custard tart are, I think, the ultimate comfort-food experiences.

Preheat the oven to 160°C/325°F/Gas Mark 3. Lightly grease or oil a 18 cm (7-inch) square × 6 cm (2½-inch) deep ceramic baking dish.

Put the milk and vanilla pod in a thick-bottomed pan and bring to the boil.

Whisk the egg yolks and castor sugar together until pale in colour.

When the milk is boiling, pour on to the egg yolks and whisk well. Strain into a large jug and keep warm.

Mix together the cake or breadcrumbs, nutmeg and zest in a large bowl. Pour on the hot milk and whisk together. Carefully pour into the prepared baking dish, cover with foil and bake for about 30 minutes. Take care when cooking, it will set and then curdle very quickly indeed: you want it just set.

When cooked, remove from the oven and cool for 15 minutes (this pudding should be eaten warm, not too hot).

Turn the oven up to 220°C/425°F/Gas Mark 7. Next, make the meringue (see page 129). Put the egg whites in a mixing bowl, add the cream of tartar and whisk on half speed. I reckon that if you beat the whites too quickly they tend to separate quicker and cannot hold their own weight. When they are thick and foamy, but not separating, add the castor sugar and whisk again on a medium speed until shiny and glossy but take care not to over whisk. Remove the bowl from the machine and carefully fold in the icing sugar.

Fit a piping bag with a 1 cm (½-inch) plain piping nozzle and then fill with the finished meringue. Pipe diagonal lines across the warm custard, leaving

a 1.5 cm (⅝-inch) gap between lines, then repeat going in the opposite direction so you end up with diamond-shaped holes.

Fill alternate holes with the two different jams and pipe a nice decoration around the edge. Sprinkle with a little castor sugar and bake in the hot oven for about 7–10 minutes, or until the pudding is a deep beige colour and the meringue is crisp. Serve with a jug of double cream.

strawberry junket
with nutmeg and clotted cream

600 ml (1 pint) whole milk

55 g (2 oz) unrefined castor sugar

7.5 ml (1½ teaspoons) rennet

225 g (8 oz) ripe English strawberries, hulled and thinly sliced

200 g (7 oz) clotted cream

2.5 ml (½ teaspoon) grated nutmeg

serves 6

This is a pudding you either love or hate. I love it, provided it is sweetened and layered with fine English strawberries and topped with clotted cream and nutmeg. An odd combination, I know, but one that works very well.

Junket is a very traditional pudding, especially in the West Country. It's made by very lightly curdling whole milk with rennet (an enzyme from a calf's stomach) at room temperature.

According to a Miss Mallock writing in her *Economics of Modern Cookery* in 1896, 'formerly a strip of calf's stomach, previously cleaned and salted, was laid in the milk to curdle it'. Thank goodness for modern technology! These days meat and vegetable rennet are available from all good chemists or pharmacies.

Heat the milk and sugar together roughly to blood temperature and then remove from the heat.

Pour into a jug, add the rennet and stir well then immediately pour into six 150 ml (¼-pint) ramekins. Leave to set at room temperature. After 1 hour, cover with cling film and chill for about an hour.

To serve, arrange the strawberries on top of the junkets. Finally, carefully top with clotted cream (this can be quite difficult as the junket is very fragile). Dust with a little nutmeg and serve.

BAKED & STEAMED
PUDDINGS

This chapter probably, more than any other, describes what we in Britain are best at. Alexis Soyer writing in his book *The Modern Housewife* (published 1849) once summed up his feelings for the great British steamed puddings by saying, 'There is hardly any of our sex, from childhood to old age but loves this truly English mixture'.

It's true: I don't know anybody who can resist a baked or steamed pudding. Every restaurant, pub or hotel menu these days has some old favourites on the menu. Spotted dick, jam roly poly, gooseberry crumble and steamed suet puddings are all very common. This is great for British food but I do have concerns that these classic puds are being upgraded and refined too far. Every supermarket, food manufacturer or whatever is trying to produce these puddings without, by the looks of it, ever having eaten one or seen an authentic recipe. I have cooked a lot of these puddings for the best part of 25 years. It takes time, care and, above all, understanding to produce them correctly.

I recently tasted a bread and butter pudding from a very well known store. It was dry, tasteless and looked appalling. The same could be said about a spotted dick that I ordered in a famous restaurant recently; again it was dry and tough as old boots, nothing like the original.

Some of the blame lies with the annual restaurant guides, whose approach to cooking and service seems to me to be formulaic and blinkered. Their grading systems pressurise chefs and cooks to cook in a certain way, rather than according to their natural talents and instincts. But chefs are not completely blameless; we find it very difficult to leave things alone. We seem hell bent on change for change's sake (I've done it myself). I'm all for refining and honing dishes if – and it's a big if – it's not detrimental to the

end product but, half the time, the end result is pretty poor.

Part of the problem lies, I think, in the fact that a lot of the most famous puddings should be served in or from the baking dish or bowl in which they are cooked. This is a fundamental part of the finished dish. A gooseberry crumble for 6–8 people with all its overcooked toffee edges, should be served at the table and spooned out. This ensures the eater gets the correct amount of crumble and filling. Then the custard or cream should be handed round. This is not only the best way to serve a pudding, but also ensures that the whole family eats and chats together.

Sussex pond pudding is another fine example. Jane Grigson once described this pudding in her book *English Food* as, 'the best of all English boiled suet puddings'. It's a suet pudding with a filling of brown sugar and butter in which whole lemons or limes are cooked. Once cooked, Sussex pond pudding should be cut at the table and shared round. Trying to adapt it for restaurant service simply does not work.

see also

fern's queen of puddings *page 22*

custard brioches *page 77*

steamed hot chocolate pudding with
    chocolate fudge sauce *page 82*

chocolate bread and butter pudding
    page 93

hot lemon and orange soufflé pudding
    page 124

baked vanilla soufflé pudding *page 127*

my mum's spotted dick

225 g (8 oz) self-raising flour
115 g (4 oz) suet
55 g (2 oz) castor sugar
85 g (3 oz) sultanas
serves 4–6

My mother always made her spotted dick this way, and my grandmother used to boil hers in a tea towel, I believe. This recipe is a classic example of a pudding that is best served by turning it out of its bowl at the table and then pouring over hot custard. My father disagrees with the latter tradition, preferring to spoon over golden syrup instead, I have to say that both are perfect accompaniments.

Place a steamer on the stove, half fill it with cold water and bring to the boil. Grease a 9 cm deep × 17 cm wide (3½ × 5½ inch) pudding basin well.

Place the flour, suet, sugar and sultanas in a bowl and add cold water until you have a dropping consistency, similar to a sponge mix. Do not overwork or the finished pudding will be heavy and chewy to eat.

Spoon into the bowl then cover well with buttered foil. Place in the steamer and steam for 2 hours, remembering to top the steamer up with boiling water from the kettle periodically.

When cooked, remove from the steamer and turn out on to a hot plate. Cover with hot custard or golden syrup and serve, simple as that and it's very good!

twice-baked toffee pudding

90 g (3 oz) unsalted butter
140 g (5 oz) unrefined castor sugar
2 large eggs, beaten
225 g (8 oz) self-raising white flour
150 g (5½ oz) plump raisins
30 ml (2 tablespoons) black treacle

for the sauce
115 g (4 oz) unsalted butter
140 g (5 oz) unrefined castor sugar
15 ml (1 tablespoon) black treacle
275 ml (9½ fl oz) double cream

serves 6–8

Apart from a steamed chocolate pudding I once encountered that had a calorie-count of 1000 calories per serving, this must be the most fattening pudding ever. That said, it is heaven to eat. I knew a gardener named Percy – he worked at the same hotel – who managed to eat three helpings of this before going to sleep it off in the orchard all afternoon; it takes no prisoners, I promise you!

The only things to eat with this are either vanilla ice cream or thick double cream; the combination of hot and cold is a real joy.

Preheat the oven to 180°C/350°F/Gas Mark 4. Well butter an 18 cm (7-inch) square baking tin.

Beat the butter and sugar together with an electric whisk, until white and fluffy. Beat in the eggs, one at a time, and don't worry if the mixture separates. Add the flour and raisins and bring together using the mixer on a low speed. Pour in 275 ml (9½ fl oz) of boiling water and then add the treacle and mix until you have a smooth batter.

Immediately pour into the baking tin and bake for about 40 minutes, or until well risen and golden. Remove from the baking tray and cool slightly.

Meanwhile, make the sauce by heating the butter, sugar, treacle and cream together in a pan. Bring to the boil and cook, whisking well, until you have a thick butterscotch sauce.

Run a knife down each side of the cooked sponge and carefully turn out on to a wire rack. Place the sponge, bottom-up, in a baking dish roughly 5 cm (2 inches) larger than the sponge itself. Carefully divide the sponge into six or eight pieces but don't cut all the way down to separate the pieces completely. Spoon over the butterscotch sauce, making sure it gets into the cuts in the sponge.

Turn down the oven to 160°C/325°F/Gas Mark 3 and bake the sponge again for 15–20 minutes, occasionally spooning the sauce over it. You will end up with a thickly-glazed sponge, with plenty of sauce around it.

Remove from the oven and leave to cool slightly before eating as it will be very hot! Alternatively, cool completely and refrigerate for up to a week. Reheat at 160–180°C/325–350°F/Gas Mark 3–4 for about 30 minutes, loosely covered with a piece of foil. You can also warm the whole dish in a microwave, again on medium setting for a couple of minutes (but check the manufacturer's instructions); cover with cling film that has been punctured several times.

bramley apple puddings

about 550 g (1 lb 4 oz) Bramley apples,
peeled, cored and cut into chunks

finely grated zest and juice of 1 lemon

60 g (2¼ oz) castor sugar

225 g (8 oz) sweet suet pastry (page 46)

beaten egg, for glazing

serves 4

I think apples are one of the most versatile fruits, especially when it comes to hot puddings. The only other fruit that comes close is rhubarb. Here is a small steamed pudding that will keep in the fridge for a week and warms up quickly in the microwave when needed. Just take care not to fill the moulds up too much – or the filling will burst out – and remember to roll the pastry nice and thinly because it will expand when it steams.

Butter four 150 ml (¼-pint) pudding moulds and four 15 cm (6-inch) double squares of foil. Place a 24 cm (9½-inch) steamer on top of a pan on the hob, fill with boiling water and keep at a simmer.

Place the apple chunks in a pan, with the lemon zest and juice and toss. Add 15 ml (1 tablespoon) of water and the sugar, and cook gently for about 10 minutes or until thick but not completely broken down. You may need to add a touch more water as the apple cooks, if the mixture looks too dry.

Meanwhile, cut the pastry into four equal pieces. Roll out one piece to about 2.5 mm (¼ inch) thick, trying to keep it as round as possible. Use the pastry to line one of the moulds. It's a bit fiddly, but press the pastry into the side of the mould, smoothing out any creases and leaving the top overhanging.

Fill the lined mould to about three-quarters full with the warm apple mixture. Trim off the top edge of pastry, leaving about 1 cm (½ inch) overhanging. Roll out the cut-off pastry to shape into a small lid and pop on top of the apples. Brush the pastry lid with beaten egg and then fold over the side pastry and press to seal. Fold the double piece of buttered foil in the centre to make a pleat. Place on top of the pudding basin and tightly wrap the pudding. Repeat to make another three puddings, then place in the steamer and cook for 35–45 minutes, or until firm and well risen. The pastry will be nice and tight in the foil top.

When cooked, remove the foil top and turn out carefully. Serve with cream or custard.

steamed jam roly-poly
with custard

225 g (8 oz) sweet suet pastry
(page 46)
185 g (6½ oz) good-quality
raspberry jam

for the custard:
500 g (1 lb 2 oz) ready-made custard or
15 g (½ oz) Bird's custard powder and
600 ml (1 pint) milk
about 55 g (2 oz) castor sugar

serves 6

This is very similar to Spotted Dick (page 29), the only thing to remember is to put plenty of jam in the roll or it will be too dry.

Have ready a 24 cm (9½-inch) diameter steamer filled with boiling water. This is very important, as the pastry should be cooked as soon as it is ready or you will end up with a heavy, leaden end-product. Cut off two pieces each of foil and baking parchment paper, measuring 40 × 40 cm (16 × 16 inches).

Roll out the pastry on a lightly floured surface to a rectangle about 30 × 37 cm (12 × 15 inches). Spread over the jam and then, starting at one of the long edges, roll up nice and lightly. Cut the roll in half so you end up with two manageable pieces.

Place one piece of baking parchment on top of a piece of foil. Sit one of the rolls on top at the edge of the parchment paper, then roll up very lightly. Twist the ends to seal and repeat with the second roll. Place in the steamer and steam for about 1 hour. To test, just gently squeeze, the rolls should be tight and firm. If not then just leave for a few more minutes.

Meanwhile, make the custard, if necessary. Mix the custard powder in a bowl with a little of the milk. Bring the rest of the milk to the boil in a pan, then carefully pour on to the custard powder mixture, whisking all the time. Return to the pan and bring to the boil, stirring all the time; remove from the heat. If using ready-made custard, just warm it in a small pan or in the microwave. Add castor sugar to taste and keep warm.

When the puddings are cooked, leave them to stand for a couple of minutes so they set slightly. Open the packages and slice each pudding into three. Serve in bowls and pour over the custard.

If you have any left over, wrap in cling film and chill. When needed, warm through in the microwave; take care, though, as the jam is prone to burning.

gooseberry crumble

875 g (1¾ lb) English gooseberries, topped and tailed
100–175 g (3½–6 oz) unrefined granulated sugar
100 g (3½ oz) cold unsalted butter, cubed
a pinch of salt
200 g (7 oz) plain white flour
100 g (3½ oz) castor sugar

serves 4

My two favourite crumbles are rhubarb and gooseberry: these puddings cannot be bettered.

Preheat the oven to 190°C/375°F/Gas Mark 5. Place the gooseberries in a stainless-steel saucepan, add the granulated sugar and heat until the fruit starts to burst. Remove from the heat and tip into a 23 cm (9-inch) ovenproof baking dish; the gooseberries should be almost in a single layer on the bottom of the dish.

Place the cold butter, salt and flour together in a food processor. Pulse until the mixture resembles fine breadcrumbs, then add the sugar and pulse again just to bring together – do not overwork (this ensures that the mixture does not 'cake up', leaving the crumble nice and loose).

Spread the crumble evenly over the cooked gooseberries and bake in the preheated oven for 20–25 minutes, or until golden. Remove from the oven and allow to cool slightly (the secret with crumble is to eat it warm, not hot) and serve with clotted cream.

steamed rhubarb pudding
with blackcurrants

400 g (14 oz) maincrop rhubarb, cut into
2 cm (¾-inch) pieces
115 g (4 oz) castor sugar
20 g (¾ oz) cornflour or arrowroot
100 g (3½ oz) fresh or frozen blackcurrants
grated zest of 1 large lemon
¾ quantity sweet suet pastry (page 46)
25 g (1 oz) cold unsalted butter, cubed

serves 6–8

The success of this pudding relies on one thing and that is to use maincrop rhubarb: the structure and flavour of this deep reddish-green, thick rhubarb suits puddings, jams, chutneys and pickling perfectly. Forced rhubarb available from January is far too delicate and best for poaching, sorbets, sauces and syrups.

The addition of a few blackcurrants give the whole pudding a nice colour and flavour.

Just make sure to keep the pastry nice and thin, remember it will expand considerably when cooked and, if you are not careful, the pudding will become dry and stodgy. Sometimes this pudding will collapse slightly and all the pink juices will flow out but this is quite normal.

Your first job is to get the steamer on and rapidly boiling. Next, lightly grease a 9 cm deep × 17 cm diameter (3½ × 5½ inches) pudding basin.

Place the rhubarb, sugar, cornflour, blackcurrants and lemon zest in a bowl and mix well.

Roll the pastry out with a rolling pin to the thickness of normal short pastry, roughly double the size of the pudding basin. Remember the pastry will swell slightly when cooked. Carefully lift the pastry and slide it into the bowl. Try to smooth out any folds in the pastry and press into the edge of the bowl lightly. Leave plenty of pastry hanging over the edge.

Spoon the rhubarb mixture into the prepared bowl and then dot with the cold butter. Fold the pastry over the top and cut away a little so you do not have such a thick layer of pastry as the lid.

Cover with a double layer of buttered foil and seal well. Place in the steamer and, cook for 2 hours, taking care to refill the steamer with boiling water every so often.

When cooked, turn out on to a warm plate and cover with warm custard and serve.

christmas pudding

115 g (4 oz) raisins

115 g (4 oz) currants

115 g (4 oz) sultanas

55 g (2 oz) chopped mixed candied peel

115 g (4 oz) carrot, coarsely grated

115 g (4 oz) cooking apple, peeled and
coarsely grated

finely grated zest of 1 orange

100 ml (3½ fl oz) cider

2 eggs, beaten

15 ml (1 tablespoon) black treacle

115 g (4 oz) muscovado sugar

115 g (4 oz) plain white flour, sifted

2.5 ml (½ teaspoon) ground mixed spice

2.5 ml (½ teaspoon) grated nutmeg

2.5 ml (½ teaspoon) ground cinnamon

115 g (4 oz) ground almonds

115 g (4 oz) vegetable suet

85 g (3 oz) bitter plain chocolate,
roughly chopped

serves 8

makes a 900 g (2 lb) pudding

As I used to live in Somerset, I know I could be accused of being biased, but I love using cider in my recipes. Here it gives extra moisture and wonderful flavour to the dried fruits and grated apple in a traditional Christmas pudding. And as if that wasn't enough, there's another secret ingredient too – chocolate!

This can be made two months ahead, stored well wrapped in foil and spiked with brandy every month. Reheat over a pan of gently simmering water or in a microwave on medium power. Serve with clotted cream, brandy butter or lashings of custard!

Grease a 1.2-litre (2-pint) pudding basin. Cut out a small circle of greaseproof paper and use to line the base.

Place the dried fruits, chopped peel, grated carrot and apple and orange zest in a large bowl, pour over the cider and allow to stand for about 10 minutes.

Add the beaten eggs, treacle and sugar to the soaked fruits and stir well to combine, then add the flour, spices, ground almonds, suet and chocolate and mix well together. Pour the mixture into the pudding basin and cover with a circle of greaseproof paper.

Place a large piece of foil on top of a large piece of greaseproof paper and then fold in the centre to make a pleat. Place the pleated papers on top of the pudding basin and use a long piece of string to tie the papers tightly just below the rim of the basin. With an extra piece of string, tie a long loop across the top – you can use this as a handle to help lower and lift the pudding in and out of the pan.

Place a heatproof saucer in the bottom of a large saucepan and sit the pudding on top. Fill the pan with enough boiling water to come halfway up the sides of the basin and then cover with a tightly fitting lid and bring the water to the boil. Reduce the heat and simmer gently for about 7–8 hours. Check the water level every couple of hours and add extra boiling water as necessary to maintain it.

PASTRIES,
PIES & TARTS

Puddings made of pastry and filled with eggs, milk, cream and honey are centuries old. Medieval cooks made a crude pastry with animal grease that they called *croste*. They called a flan tin lined with pastry, a *coffin of paast*. These were filled with all sorts of fruit and nut combinations, but by far the most popular were fillings of eggs, cream and milk.

Pastry is still the basis of many savoury and sweet flans, pies and other puddings. In fact hardly a day goes by without hearing of a new type of pastry. Most of these are variations on the basic theme of flour, fat and liquid, maybe with some sort of flavouring such as nutmeg, citrus zest or cocoa.

Yet I don't think any other part of the pastry chef's craft

has attracted so many old wives tales as pastry-making. Let me just refresh your memory with three real gems: *chill the flour and cut fat overnight*; *sift the flour to help lighten the pastry*; and the best one of all, *only people with cold hands can make good pastry*. What a load of rubbish! Firstly, as long as the fat is cold and you work quickly, there is no problem. Secondly, sifting flour makes absolutely no difference whatsoever to the lightness of the finished pastry. For light pastry you need the correct proportion of fat to flour; you need the steam which the liquid provides; and most importantly you mustn't overwork the dough in the way you would for bread.

So, the rules are simple: very cold fat; chill the finished pastry before rolling out; don't overwork (especially with a rolling pin); and finally, never roll out the finished pastry more than twice. I once worked with a lady called Cissy and she had a great saying: 'Treat pastry with respect, and you will be fine'.

Finally, I couldn't write this chapter without mentioning bought pastry. Over the years much scorn has been poured on 'ready-made food' a lot of it rightly. But there are exceptions. Frozen peas are a classic and good-quality pastry is another. Ask yourself, 'Can I make it any better?' If you can't, buy it. What's wrong with that? Most chefs can't make pastry to save their lives. The selection of ready-made pastry available today is vast and very good indeed. The only rule I make is to use all-butter puff pastry. This has a far superior flavour than the variety with shortening.

techniques

Filling a pastry case with a liquid filling

Where you have a flan that is filled with a liquid, custard-style filling that needs to be baked until set, it is very easy to slop some of the filling over the side of the flan, where it can stick the pastry to the side of the flan ring making it impossible to get the flan out of the tin. On the other hand, these flans need to be filled right to the top for the best look and taste. If the custard is too shallow it will overcook and be dry.

To avoid both these problems, put the flan case still in its tin and resting on a baking sheet in the preheated oven and carefully pull out the oven shelf. Fill the pastry three-quarters full with the filling and gently slide the shelf back into the oven. Finally, use an egg cup to fill the flan up to the very top with the rest of the mixture.

Remember not to overcook these types of flans; the filling should still be slightly wobbly in the centre. It's very difficult to put a time on this as ovens vary, so keep an eye on the tart as it will overcook very quickly indeed and soufflé (puff up) at the edges.

Glazing a custard-filled flan

Glazing a custard-filled flan under the grill is difficult, because the heat of the grill can overcook the filling causing it to become grainy. The best way is to use a culinary blowtorch. When the flan is cool, sprinkle with a fine layer of icing sugar through a sieve and glaze with the blowtorch. For a nice, even glaze, repeat this process.

The same method can, of course, be applied to crème brûlées of all sorts.

see also

bitter chocolate tart *page 84*
chocolate puff pastry slice *page 90*
fresh strawberry mille-feuille *page 265*
baby bakewells with lime water icing
   page 281

sweet shortcrust pastry
and blind-baking a flan

115 g (4 oz) cold unsalted butter, cubed

225 g (8 oz) plain white flour

a pinch of salt

10 ml (2 teaspoons) castor sugar

1 egg, lightly beaten, plus extra to glaze

half an eggshell full of cold water

makes enough to

line a 23 cm (9-inch) diameter, 3 cm

(1½-inch) deep, fluted flan ring

This is a basic pastry to be used for any dessert work. The method of lining the flan ring is roughly the same for all sizes and shapes.

Place the cold butter, flour, salt and sugar together in a food processor. Blitz until you have a fine breadcrumb texture but do not overwork. Add the egg and water and mix well, using the pulse button; again, do not overwork or the pastry will shrink when cooked. Turn out of the processor and knead very gently, just to bring together. Flatten slightly (this makes it easier to roll when chilled) and wrap in cling film, then chill for about 20 minutes.

Lightly flour the surface on which you are going to roll the pastry. Roll the pastry out so you end up with a circle about 4 cm (1¾ inches) larger all round than the flan ring. Carefully roll the pastry on to the rolling pin and then unroll over the flan ring, taking care not stretch the pastry too much.

Immediately ease the pastry into the ring and gently push into the bottom and corners; try to make sure that you do not leave any creases in the outside. Use your thumb to push the pastry into the fluted tin, leaving about 1 cm (½ inch) overhanging the top edge. Then trim off with a sharp knife or roll a rolling pin over the top to remove the excess. Thumb up the top edge again and pinch with your thumb and forefinger to make the edge more decorative; this will also help to stop the pastry from shrinking back into the tin (remember, the higher the rim the more filling you can have in the finished tart, flan or pie). Using a piece of well floured leftover pastry, push the bottom of the flan into the corners so it's nice and flush. Prick well with a fork and chill for 30 minutes.

Preheat the oven to 200°C/400°F/Gas Mark 6. Cut out a piece of greaseproof paper roughly 4 cm (2 inches) larger than the flan, scrunch it up, then flatten it out again and carefully place inside the lined flan tin. Fill with baking beans and bake for about 15 minutes, or until the top edge is slightly brown. Remove the paper and beans, turn the oven down to 160°C/325°F/Gas Mark 3 and cook for a further 10 minutes until the pastry is set but has taken no colour. Remove from the oven, brush with beaten egg (this prevents the pastry from getting soggy when you add the filling) and then pop back into the oven for 2 minutes to seal. Cool for a little while before adding the filling.

cocoa pastry

100 g (3½ oz) unrefined castor sugar

a pinch of salt

175 g (6 oz) unsalted butter, softened

1 egg, lightly beaten

300 g (10½ oz) plain white flour, sifted

15 g (½ oz) cocoa powder, sifted

makes enough to

line a 23 cm (9-inch) diameter

3 cm (1½-inch) fluted deep flan tin

This makes a nice change from the ordinary shortcrust pastry used in flans and pies, such as Bitter Chocolate Tart (page 84).

Cream together the sugar, salt and butter until pale and then gradually beat in the egg. Finally, mix in the flour and cocoa powder, briefly knead the dough into a ball and then flatten it slightly.

Wrap in cling film and chill for 1 hour before using.

Unwrap, roll out and use as for sweet shortcrust pastry (opposite).

puff pastry

415 g (14½ oz) cold, unsalted butter

450 g (1 lb) strong white flour,
plus extra to dust

2 pinches of salt

about 175 ml (6 fl oz) very cold water

30 ml (2 tablespoons) lemon juice

makes

about 1 kg (2¼ lb)

It took me the best part of two years to make puff pastry successfully but now this, and making croissants, are my two all-time-favourite jobs in the kitchen. There is something really satisfying about producing great pastry. Just follow the recipe closely as there is really no margin for error.

Cut 115 g (4 oz) of the butter into small cubes and allow the rest of the butter to soften slightly at cool room temperature (watch out if the kitchen is hot in summer months). Place the flour, salt and cubed butter in a food mixer or processor and make fine breadcrumbs. Add the water and lemon juice and mix to a dough – the dough should be firm but not too firm.

Remove the dough from the machine and knead into a flattened ball. Roll out with a rolling pin to 35 × 45 cm (14 × 18 inches) – this may be a little difficult but persevere. Place on a floured tray, cover with cling film and chill for at least 30 minutes.

Meanwhile, cut out a piece of greaseproof paper roughly 30 × 20 cm (12 × 8 inches). Cut the remaining butter lengthways into six slices and lay evenly out on to the greaseproof paper. Use a palette knife to merge the butter together and cover the paper. This process will make the first – and the most critical – rolling-out easier. Leave the butter in a cool place.

Remove the dough from the fridge and check it is soft enough to roll – by this I mean that while the dough was very taut when mixed in the machine, it should have relaxed sufficiently in the fridge that there is little resistance when pulled apart with your fingers. If the dough is too stiff still, just leave it to relax for a little longer. If the dough is too stiff then you will not be able to roll it out easily; on the other hand, if the dough is too slack (due to too much water) the butter will push through when the rolling process starts, losing all the raising layers of butter and pastry.

When it comes to adding butter to the dough for the first time, make sure that they are both the same temperature. Lightly flour a board or worktop and lay the dough on top. Place the spread butter on one half of the dough, by inverting the greaseproof on to the dough and peeling it off, then fold the opposite side over the butter to enclose it and seal well. This is very important: I fold the two layers on to themselves making a tight seal – if this seal is broken then the butter will squeeze out and ruin the pastry.

Now carefully roll out the pastry in one direction until it is roughly three times as long as the original piece, making sure all the corners are square and you have a true oblong shape. Dust off excess flour and fold the pastry into three.

Twist the pastry through 90° and mark an arrow in the pastry in the original rolling direction, so you know which direction to roll next time – you must make sure you do this after each turn as this will ensure that the pastry rises evenly when finally cooked. Chill well for 30 minutes to relax.

Repeat the rolling and folding process a further five times, ensuring you dust off excess flour each time, take care to ensure the corners are square and that the pastry is turned and arrowed in the same direction. Between each rolling, cover with cling film and chill for at least 30 minutes.

Roll out the finished pastry and use as required. This will freeze perfectly in its raw state, just wrap well and defrost overnight.

choux pastry

115 g (4 oz) unsalted butter, cubed

a pinch of sugar

a pinch of salt

140 g (5 oz) plain white flour, sifted

3–4 large eggs, beaten

makes enough for

about 70 baby éclairs

I always found this pastry difficult to make but then, one day, I think I found out the reason. When you boil the water, if the butter is in large cubes you tend to get quite a bit of evaporation before the fat is completely melted. This changes the proportion of water to butter; you end up with the wrong balance so the cooked pastry will not fully rise when cooked. So make sure the butter is cut into very small pieces and you should be fine!

Bring the butter and 300 ml (½ pint) of cold water to the boil in a pan. Add the sugar and salt, and then straight away add the flour and beat well until the mixture comes away from the pan. Allow to cool completely (more egg is absorbed when the mixture is cold).

Gradually add three of the beaten eggs to the cooled pastry, a little at a time (if you can, it's best to do this in a food mixer, or food processor) and then beat small amounts of the last egg into the mixture until you get the right consistency. The reason for only adding three of the eggs at the start is that the mixture needs to be quite tight; if you add too much egg the end product will not rise correctly and, of course, you can always add the extra egg but you can't take it out. If the paste is to be used for fritters or beignets then it has to be fairly tight. The finished paste should just fall off the paddle on the machine. It's best to use choux dough straight away but it will keep for a couple of days in the fridge.

shortbread pastry
pâte sablé

200 g (7 oz) unsalted butter

a pinch of salt

100 g (3½ oz) golden, unrefined
castor sugar

1 large egg yolk

250 g (9 oz) plain white flour

makes enough for

two 23 cm (9-inch) diameter × 4 cm
(1¾-inch) deep flan rings

This pastry is suitable for flans, fruit pies, Bakewell tarts, biscuits and even very rich mince pies. It's a very rich and crumbly pastry that can be quite temperamental to handle but is really good for some desserts, such as sponge-filled tarts. Stick to shortcrust when you have a large amount of liquid filling, such as an egg-custard tart.

Beat the butter, salt and castor sugar together in a bowl with a wooden spoon until just soft. Add the egg yolk and flour and mix to make a stiff dough. Remove from the bowl, wrap in cling film and chill for 20 minutes.

Roll out as for shortcrust pastry (page 40). Do take care to roll out quickly as the butter rapidly warms up, making it difficult to work with.

Always cook in a fairly hot oven so the butter sets sharpish or the pastry will collapse.

sweet suet pastry

225 g (8 oz) self-raising white flour

a pinch of salt

115 g (4 oz) suet

55 g (2 oz) castor sugar

1 egg

about 60 ml (4 tablespoons) cold water

makes enough to make

four 150 ml (¼-pint) puddings or

two 15 cm (6-inch) rolls

Place the flour, salt, suet, sugar and egg in a bowl and mix well. Add a little of the water at a time until you have a soft, but not sticky, dough.

Roll out on a lightly floured surface and use straight away as the raising agents start working immediately.

gooseberry tart

2 × 300 g cans of gooseberries or 400 g
(14 oz) freshly poached gooseberries,
well drained
4 large eggs plus 2 large egg yolks
140 g (5 oz) castor sugar
225 ml (8 fl oz) whipping cream
juice of 1 small lime
25 cm (10-inch) diameter × 4 cm
(1¾-inch) deep sweet shortcrust pastry
case, baked blind (page 40)

serves 6–8

Fresh gooseberry purée is an absolute joy; gooseberry is the first of the glorious summer berries and gets you in the mood for what's to come. The fact that gooseberries are only around for a few weeks makes them all the more special. I used to bottle my own, a job that takes a little time but is well worth the effort. Canned gooseberries in syrup are actually quite a good substitute for a tart like this, but do make sure you buy a good-quality brand – I find Hartley's is the best.

Preheat the oven to 160°C/325°F/Gas Mark 3. Blitz the gooseberries in a liquidiser until you have a thick purée. Press through a fine sieve.

Whisk the eggs and egg yolks in a bowl with the sugar and cream until smooth. Add the gooseberry purée and whisk carefully – the mixture will thicken but don't worry, if you continue to whisk the mixture will let itself down again. Finally add the lime juice and then pour into the cooked pastry case (see page 39). Bake for about 40–45 minutes, or until just set.

Leave to cool to room temperature. Slice and serve with vanilla ice cream.

egg custard tart
with blackcurrant sauce

500 ml (18 fl oz) whipping cream

1 vanilla pod, split

6 egg yolks

85 g (3 oz) castor sugar

5 ml (1 teaspoon) arrowroot

5 ml (1 teaspoon) rose-water

19 cm (7½-inch) diameter × 5 cm (2-inch) deep sweet shortcrust pastry case, baked blind (page 40)

10 ml (2 teaspoons) grated nutmeg

icing sugar, sifted, to decorate

for the blackcurrant sauce

300 g (10½ oz) frozen blackcurrants

100 g (3½ oz) castor sugar

a squeeze of lemon juice

serves 6–8

This is probably the most frequently cooked and eaten dessert I have ever made, it was always a real winner with diners.

Preheat the oven to 160°C/325°F/Gas Mark 3. Pour the cream into a small pan, add the vanilla pod and bring to the boil.

Meanwhile, whisk the egg yolks and sugar together for 1 minute, and then whisk in the arrowroot. Pour on the boiling cream and stir well, add the rose-water and strain the whole mixture through a fine sieve.

Pour the cream and egg mixture into the pastry case (see page 39) and carefully place in the oven. Cook for about 30 minutes, or until just set and still slightly wobbly (the custard can suddenly overcook so keep an eye on the oven). When cooked remove from the oven, sprinkle over the nutmeg and leave to cool. Chill well, preferably overnight.

To make the blackcurrant sauce, liquidise the blackcurrants with the sugar, lemon juice and about 75 ml (5 tablespoons) of cold water to make a smooth sauce, adding a touch more water if needed. Pass through a fine sieve to remove any seeds.

To serve, cut the tart into 6–8 nice wedges, dust with icing sugar and pour over a little blackcurrant sauce.

glazed passion-fruit
and orange tart

12 ripe passion-fruit, halved

8 eggs

250 g (9 oz) castor sugar

a pinch of cornflour

600 ml (1 pint) double cream

finely grated zest of 1 large orange

25 cm (10-inch) diameter × 4 cm

(1¾-inch) deep sweet shortcrust

pastry case, baked blind (page 40)

sifted golden icing sugar, to glaze

serves 6–8

This is one of my favourite puddings, fairly simple to prepare and delicious to eat. It's an afternoon-tea favourite but also fits well into any dinner or lunch party. I quite like to serve this tart with some freshly picked English strawberries or raspberries at room temperature.

The glazing is best done with a small, powerful blowtorch, it's very difficult to glaze this kind of pastry tart with a creamy, just-set filling under the grill without curdling the custard; so if you do not own a blowtorch, just dust with unrefined icing sugar.

Preheat the oven to 180°C/350°F/Gas Mark 4. Scoop out all the flesh and pulp from the passion-fruit. The next step is to remove the juice from the pips – I use a hand blender set on the lowest speed so all the flesh comes away very easily. The trouble with a liquidiser is that the high speed breaks up the seeds so you end up with a custard with black specks; you can avoid this to some extent by using the pulse setting. Failing all of these, push the passion-fruit pulp through a fine sieve. Place the passion-fruit juice and flesh in a measuring jug – you should end up with just over 200 ml (7 fl oz) of juice (top it up with orange juice if it's a bit short).

Put the eggs, sugar and cornflour in a large bowl and whisk well but do not overwork. Pour in the double cream, passion-fruit juice and orange zest and mix well (the mixture will slightly curdle but don't panic, just keep on gently whisking and it will thin out again).

Pour the filling into the pastry case (see page 39) and cook for about 45 minutes or until the custard is just set but still wobbly – it's very difficult to put an exact time on this so keep an eye on the tart as it will overcook very quickly indeed and 'soufflé' up at the edges. Carefully remove from the oven and cool on a wire rack.

To serve, dust with a small amount of sifted golden icing sugar and glaze with a blowtorch, then repeat this process to ensure a nice, even glaze (see page 39). Cut into wedges and serve with a large blob of very lightly whipped double cream.

This tart will keep for one day in a fridge but is best eaten fresh at room temperature within a couple of hours of cooking.

melon and mint tart

1 ripe Galia or 2 small Charentais melons, about 1.1 kg (2 lb 7 oz) total weight

100–200 ml (3½–7 fl oz) Sauvignon Blanc white wine

20 ml (4 teaspoons) castor sugar

2 pinches of citric acid powder

8 fresh mint leaves, finely chopped (optional)

2½ gelatine leaves, soaked in cold water

23 cm (9-inch) diameter × 4 cm (1½-inch) deep sweet shortcrust pastry case, baked blind (page 40)

serves 4–6

A very refreshing tart that really has to be eaten fairly quickly. The best thing is to chill it very well and serve with cream. This is a good pudding to serve after a heavy meal, or it's just fine with a cup of tea.

Cut the melon or melons in half and scoop out the seeds with a spoon. Next, using a 2 cm (¾-inch) melon baller, scoop out as many melon balls as possible and keep to one side.

Scoop out all the flesh that is left on the skin and place in a liquidiser, along with 100 ml (3½ fl oz) of the white wine, the castor sugar, citric acid and mint leaves, if using. Blitz until smooth and then pass through a fine sieve and pour into a measuring jug. You will need 400 ml (14 fl oz) in total, if you have slightly less just top up with a little more white wine.

Remove the gelatine from the water and shake off any excess, then place in a small pan and gently heat until melted.

Quickly stir the melted gelatine into the melon purée, add the melon balls and stir well. Pour into the cooked flan case, arrange the melon balls so the rounded sides are uppermost and then chill for about 2 hours, or until set.

Cut into wedges and serve with cream.

plum tart

375 g (13 oz) puff pastry (page 42) or a
375 g sheet of 'all-butter' ready-rolled
puff pastry
1 large egg yolk
50 g (1¾ oz) white bread (about 2 slices),
crusts removed and crumb made
into fine breadcrumbs
600 g (1 lb 5 oz) ripe plums (about 10),
halved and stoned
20 g (¾ oz) castor sugar
45 ml (3 tablespoons) apricot jam

serves 4–6

A nice way to use plums not often seen these days. My old pastry chef used to cook a version of this using the small mirabelles from France and serve it as an afternoon-tea fancy. Nice with a large cup of Earl Grey.

Preheat the oven to 200°C/400°F/Gas Mark 6. Lay the pastry out on a non-stick baking sheet and trim so you end up with a sheet measuring 23 cm (9 inches) × 30 cm (12 inches).

Break up the egg yolk with a pastry brush and brush a 3 cm (1½-inch) border of egg all around the edge of the sheet, taking care not too let the egg spill over the cut edge as it can impede the rising of the pastry.

Then, with a sharp knife and going only halfway through the thickness of the pastry, not all the way through, make an incision marking out a 2 cm (¾-inch) border all around the pastry – this will allow the sides to rise up around the plums. Prick all over the centre of the pastry with a fork.

Spread the breadcrumbs over the pastry but keep them off the border. Lay the halved plums on top of the breadcrumbs, again keeping inside the incision. Sprinkle the sugar over the plums.

Bake for 30 minutes, or until well risen and golden. Remove from the oven and leave to cool.

Mix the jam and 15 ml (1 tablespoon) of water together and then bring to the boil. Brush the whole tart with the warmed apricot jam and cut into slices.

semolina and lavender tart

with apricots and pine nuts

115 g (4 oz) unrefined castor sugar

115 g (4 oz) unsalted butter

2 large eggs, beaten

25 g (1 oz) potato flour

115 g (4 oz) semolina

finely grated zest of 1 large lemon

30 ml (2 tablespoons) dried
lavender (optional)

24 cm (9½-inch) diameter × 4 cm
(1¾-inch) deep sweet shortcrust pastry
case, baked blind (page 40)

100 g (3½ oz) pine nuts

2 × 410 g cans of apricot halves, drained

icing sugar, to decorate

200 g (7 oz) greek-style yogurt, to serve

serves 6–8

It's not often you see semolina used in this way: most people remember it as the awful, sticky gunge dished out at school mealtimes. This is a novel and interesting way to use this forgotten-about sixties pudding staple. The inclusion of lavender is up to you. I pick ours each year, dry it, and then store it in an airtight container. It keeps very well.

Preheat the oven to 180°C/350°F/Gas Mark 4. Cream the sugar and butter together until light and fluffy and then add the eggs, a little at a time, until fully incorporated. Fold in the potato flour, semolina, lemon zest and lavender, if using, but do not overwork. Spoon into the blind-baked pastry case and spread out evenly.

Sprinkle over the pine nuts and arrange half the apricots evenly over the top, keeping the rounded side uppermost. Bake in the oven for 30–40 minutes or until set and well risen.

Remove from the oven and allow to cool. Dust heavily with icing sugar and carefully glaze under a hot grill or with a blowtorch.

Roughly chop the remaining apricots, add to the yogurt and stir well. Serve with a large wedge of the flan and a cup of Earl Grey tea.

peach and almond tart

85 g (3 oz) flaked almonds

4 large, ripe peaches

23 cm (9-inch) diameter × 3 cm
(1½-inch) deep sweet shortcrust
pastry case, baked blind (page 40)

2 large egg yolks

200 ml (7 fl oz) double cream

60 g (2¼ oz) unrefined castor sugar

30 ml (2 tablespoons) brandy, preferably
peach flavoured

unrefined icing sugar, to decorate

serves 6–8

This tart must be eaten at room temperature to get the best flavour, all you will need to go with it is a little very thick cream.

Preheat the oven to 180°C/350°F/Gas Mark 4 and bake the almonds for about 5–6 minutes until lightly browned. Bring a small pan of water to the boil. Once boiling, drop the peaches in, one at a time, leave for 10 seconds and then straight away lift out with a slotted spoon and plunge into a bowl of iced water. You will find the skins should come away now very easily; if not, just repeat the process.

Place the browned almonds in the bottom of the cooked tart case. Cut each peach into twelve slices and arrange on top of the almonds.

Whisk the egg yolks, cream, castor sugar and brandy together and pour over the sliced peaches. Sit the pastry case on a baking sheet and cook in the oven for about 30 minutes, or until the custard is just set. Remove from the oven and leave to cool.

Just before serving, dust with a little unrefined icing sugar and glaze under a hot grill or with a blowtorch (see page 39). Serve at room temperature, with thick cream.

macadamia nut tart

325 g (11½ oz) macadamia nuts

85 g (3 oz) golden castor sugar

50 ml (2 fl oz) double cream

50 ml (2 fl oz) acacia honey

or golden syrup

a pinch of salt

finely grated zest of 1 lemon

10 ml (2 teaspoons) vanilla powder

or extract

3 large egg yolks

85 g (3 oz) unsalted butter, melted and warm

24 cm (9½-inch) diameter × 4 cm

(1¾-inch) deep sweet shortcrust pastry

case, baked blind (page 40)

serves 6–8

The macadamia nut is synonymous with Australia but in fact is now grown in the United States and other countries. I believe it is one of the world's most expensive nuts and is very high in natural fats, something like 70%. Nevertheless, macadamias are absolutely gorgeous. The only way to eat them, I think, is in a warm tart with honey and brown sugar.

Preheat the oven to 200°C/400°F/Gas Mark 6 and toast the macadamias for 6–8 minutes or until lightly browned. Turn the oven down to 160°C/325°F/Gas Mark 3 Roughly chop the toasted macadamias, not too small.

Stir together the castor sugar, cream, honey or syrup, salt, lemon zest, vanilla powder or extract and egg yolks. Stir in the warm melted butter and bring together.

Pour into the blind-baked pastry case and bake for 35 minutes, or until just set. Allow to cool before slicing and serve with a little ice cream or crème fraîche.

baked raspberry tart

500 g (1 lb 2 oz) fresh ripe summer
raspberries

70 g (2½ oz) unrefined castor sugar

juice and finely grated zest of 1 large lemon

25 cm (10-inch) diameter × 4 cm
(1¾-inch) deep sweet shortcrust pastry
case, baked blind (page 40)

5 ml (1 teaspoon) ground cinnamon

serves 6–8

I don't, as a rule, like to cook summer berries, to me they are just perfect on their own, served at room temperature with cream. But here we have a nice summer lunchtime dessert that's a little different and very simple.

Preheat the oven to 190°C/375°F/Gas Mark 5. Place the raspberries, sugar, lemon juice and zest in a pan and then heat just to bring to the boil, stirring occasionally but trying not to break the fruit up too much.

Straight away pour the cooked raspberries into the tart case, which they should fill right to the brim. Sprinkle over the ground cinnamon and bake for 35 minutes, or until thick and just set. Remove from the oven and allow to cool completely.

Serve at room temperature, cut into thick slices, with a nice blob of crème fraîche.

rhubarb and almond
crumble tart

175 g (6 oz) granulated sugar

300 g (10½ oz) maincrop rhubarb,
washed well and cut into 2.5 cm
(1-inch) pieces

for the sponge

115 g (4 oz) very soft unsalted butter

115 g (4 oz) castor sugar

2 eggs, beaten

25 g (1 oz) plain white flour, sifted

115 g (4 oz) ground almonds

23 cm (9-inch) diameter × 4 cm
(1½-inch) deep sweet shortcrust pastry
case, baked blind (page 40)

for the crumble

115 g (4 oz) plain white flour

140 g (5 oz) cold unsalted butter, cubed

85 g (3 oz) granulated sugar

55 g (2 oz) Jordan's Original Muesli

55 g (2 oz) porridge oats

serves 4–6

This recipe uses maincrop rhubarb, the deep red, olive-green-tipped variety. This is grown outside and most gardens have a few crowns. Ready to eat from March right through to May and a lot more stringy than forced rhubarb, it is nevertheless perfect for this tart.

You could use the indoor, forced variety for this but it has such a delicate flavour that it might get lost in the sponge.

Preheat the oven to 180°C/350°F/Gas Mark 4. Dissolve the sugar in 175 ml (6 fl oz) of cold water and then add the rhubarb and bring to the boil. Once boiling, turn the heat right down and simmer very gently for about 1 minute – do not overcook, the rhubarb needs to be kept whole. Cover and leave to cool completely.

To make the sponge, cream the butter and sugar together until thick and creamy. Slowly add the eggs, beating all the time. When fully incorporated gently fold in the flour and almonds.

Spoon the mixture into the prepared pastry case and then top with the strained, cooled, poached rhubarb. Bake for about 25 minutes.

Meanwhile make the crunchy, crumble topping. Pop the flour and butter into a food processor and blend into fine breadcrumbs. Then add the sugar and mix well. Add the muesli and porridge oats and pulse briefly just to mix together.

When the tart is starting to brown and just set, fill the tart with the crumble topping, making sure that the topping is proud of the top of the pastry case. Pop into the oven again and continue to cook for about a further 20 minutes. The topping will turn golden brown and nice and crunchy.

Remove from the oven and leave to cool for 15–20 minutes before you eat, I think it's best to leave until just warm. Serve with cream or custard.

fresh strawberry, mint
and pistachio tart

250 g (9 oz) cream cheese

30 ml (2 tablespoons) unrefined castor sugar

grated zest and juice of 1 small orange

15 ml (1 tablespoon) chopped fresh mint

23 cm (9-inch) diameter × 2.5 cm
(1-inch) deep sweet shortcrust
pastry case, baked blind (page 40)

500 g (1 lb 2 oz) small English
strawberries, hulled

90 ml (6 tablespoons) strawberry jam

60 ml (4 tablespoons) chopped,
peeled pistachios

There is something very attractive about this flan; the deep red of the strawberries and the glaze, contrasting with the deep green of the pistachios, looks stunning. Just remember to use ripe, room-temperature English strawberries.

Beat together the cream cheese, sugar and orange zest and then carefully mix in the orange juice and mint.

Spread the cheese mixture over the bottom of the pastry case. Top with the strawberries, packing them tightly together.

Heat the strawberry jam with 45 ml (3 tablespoons) of cold water, stirring all the time. Sieve the jam mixture and then carefully spoon over the strawberries making sure it covers them all. Sprinkle with the chopped pistachios and leave to cool. Serve with lightly whipped double cream.

pecan pie

175 g (6 oz) pecans (or walnuts,
it's up to you)

25 g (1 oz) bitter chocolate, grated

2.5 ml (½ teaspoon) vanilla powder
or extract

2 pinches of salt

175 g (6 oz) good-quality maple syrup

2 large eggs

150 g (5½ oz) golden granulated sugar

55 g (2 oz) butter, melted

24 cm (9½-inch) diameter × 4 cm
(1¾-inch) deep, sweet shortcrust pastry
case, baked blind (page 40)

serves 8

One of the better things to come out of America, this is a truly great dessert. I often wonder how anyone came to invent this pie: it has to have been a mistake because, when you look at how the thing is put together, you think it surely can't work! But work it does and, as I have said, it's a marvel when it is made properly.

The American versions I have tasted over there, have always been tooth-achingly sweet; my version is less sweet, just serve with cream or on its own with a cup of tea.

Preheat the oven to 160°C/325°F/Gas Mark 3. Place the nuts, chocolate, vanilla, salt and maple syrup in a bowl.

Beat the eggs together and stir into the nut mixture, with the sugar. Finally, add the melted butter and stir well.

Pour into the prepared pastry case and bake for 40–50 minutes or until set in the middle. Allow to cool completely before trying to cut.

prune and brandy
meringue pie

420 g can of prunes in syrup,
drained and stoned
30 ml (2 tablespoons) brandy or Armagnac
2 large eggs plus 2 large egg yolks
300 ml (10 fl oz) whipping cream
50 g (1¾ oz) castor sugar
a squeeze of lemon juice
24 cm (9½-inch) diameter × 4 cm
(1¾-inch) deep sweet shortcrust pastry
case, baked blind (page 40)

for the meringue
3 large egg whites
a pinch of cream of tartar
85 g (3 oz) castor sugar
85 g (3 oz) icing sugar
granulated sugar, to decorate

serves 6–8

A great combination using canned prunes; the pie is very tasty and a complete change from the normal lemon meringue pie.

Preheat the oven to 180°C/350°F/Gas Mark 4. Place the stoned prunes and brandy or Armagnac in a liquidiser and blitz to make a very thick purée.

Spoon the purée into a bowl, add the eggs and yolks and mix well. Add the cream, sugar and lemon juice and whisk until smooth.

Pour into the blind-baked pastry base (see page 39). Place on a baking sheet and cook in the oven for about 35 minutes or until just set – the pie should be slightly wobbly right in the centre when the pie is tapped, this is perfect as the residual heat will finish off the pie. Do not let the pie overcook or 'soufflé' or it will separate. When cooked, remove from the oven.

Turn up the oven to 220°C/425°F/Gas Mark 7. Make the meringue by whisking the egg whites and cream of tartar on a moderate speed until thick and creamy (see page 129). Add the castor sugar and continue to whisk until thick and glossy. Finally add the icing sugar and whisk well.

Pipe the meringue decoratively on to the top of the pie, sprinkle over a little granulated sugar and bake in the hot oven for a few minutes until the meringue is firm to the touch and lightly browned.

coconut tart

2 × 50 g sachets of creamed coconut

600 ml (1 pint) whipping cream

8 egg yolks

115 g (4 oz) castor sugar

45 ml (3 tablespoons) Malibu
coconut liqueur

24 cm (9½-inch) diameter × 4 cm
(1¾-inch) deep sweet shortcrust pastry
case, baked blind (page 40)

100 g (3½ oz) desiccated coconut, toasted
in the oven until crunchy

serves 6–8

This is a variation of my all-time-favourite pudding, egg custard tart. It is very difficult to get people to eat coconut – most are put off by being force-fed Auntie Betty's coconut buns, or rock-hard macaroons, when they were small children, I can't really blame them, desiccated coconut isn't the nicest thing to eat. But if it is used carefully and with a little thought, as with most 'difficult' ingredients, the results can be very good.

This creamy tart is very moreish and perfect on a summer's day with a little fresh fruit and a coconut or mango sorbet (page 198 or 193).

Preheat the oven to 160°C/325°F/Gas Mark 3. Pour 300 ml (½ pint) of boiling water on to the creamed coconut and stir to dissolve.

Pour the cream into a saucepan and bring to the boil. Meanwhile, whisk together (by hand so the egg does not froth up too much) the egg yolks and sugar. Pour on the boiling cream and mix well. Add the Malibu and coconut milk and mix well.

Place the flan case on a baking sheet and pour in the filling (see page 39). Cook for about 30 minutes, checking occasionally that the filling is not puffing up and spoiling, if this starts to happen you may need to turn the oven down a touch.

When cooked the tart must still have what we call 'the wobble factor', this means it just wobbles when the side of the tray is tapped. Remove from the oven and place on a wire rack.

Sprinkle over the toasted coconut very carefully and then leave to cool completely. Chill well, if possible overnight. Cut into large wedges to serve.

twice-cooked rhubarb tart

225 g (8 oz) puff pastry (page 42) or 225 g (8 oz) sheet of all-butter ready-rolled puff pastry (25 cm/10-inch disc)
450 g (1 lb) new-season rhubarb, trimmed and cut into 5 cm (2-inch) pieces
juice of 1 large lemon
200 g (7 oz) castor sugar
55 g (2 oz) unsalted butter

serves 4

The only way to cook rhubarb tart this way is to pre-cook the rhubarb, or you end up with too much juice and soggy pastry. This is a very simple pudding but very tasty and quick to prepare. It is best to use new-season rhubarb for this dish as maincrop rhubarb would be too stringy.

Roll out the pastry very thinly to a 30 cm (12-inch) circle and chill for 30 minutes.

Preheat the oven to 220°C/425°F/Gas Mark 7. Place the rhubarb, half the lemon juice and 85 g (3 oz) of the sugar in a pan and gently cook for about 4–5 minutes, or until the rhubarb is just soft but still whole. Carefully strain through a colander.

Next, prick the puff pastry well with a fork.

Place the remaining 115 g (4 oz) of castor sugar in an ovenproof 25 cm (10-inch) diameter non-stick frying pan. Heat the sugar until it turns to a light caramel and then stir in the butter – at this point it looks like the whole thing is separating but don't panic, this is quite normal. Add the rest of the lemon juice and stir; the sauce will start to thicken again.

Arrange the well drained rhubarb in the hot pan and then immediately lay the pastry on top of the bubbling, buttery caramel and rhubarb mixture. Using a round-bladed knife, tuck the edges of the pastry down the sides of the pan. Let the pan bubble away for about 2–3 minutes and then put the pan in the hot oven and cook for about 12–14 minutes, depending on the thickness of the pastry. When the pastry is well risen and a nice golden colour, remove from the oven and leave to set for 3 minutes before attempting to turn it out. This allows the sauce to thicken and it will hold its shape better.

Carefully turn out by placing a plate on top of the pan and invert quickly, be careful of any hot sauce which may spill out. Cut into wedges and serve with cream or ice cream.

mince pies

400 g (14 oz) unsalted butter, softened

a pinch of salt

2.5 ml (½ teaspoon) ground mixed spice

200 g (7 oz) castor sugar

finely grated zest of 2 oranges

3 large egg yolks

500 g (1 lb 2 oz) plain white flour, sifted

450 g (1 lb) luxury mincemeat

1 large egg, beaten, to glaze

brown sugar, to sprinkle

makes 20–24

There are numerous ways of making mince pies – in patty tins, on baking sheets and using shortbread, shortcrust or even puff pastry. My favourite method and, I think, the most delicious, is using patty tins and the pastry recipe below – they're crumbly, buttery and a perfect treat for teatime on Boxing Day.

I really think that, if you are too busy to make your own mincemeat, buying a good-quality product is fine; there are some very good ones around these days.

Because of the high proportion of butter to flour, this pastry is very short and crumbly. At room temperature the dough is rather fragile and will soften quickly, so it is important that it is well chilled before you attempt to work with it. When rolling out, handle only the amount of pastry you need at that time and leave the remainder in the fridge.

For the same reason, allow the mince pies to cool before removing from the tins so the butter has a chance to firm up.

Place the softened butter in a large mixing bowl with the salt, mixed spice, castor sugar and orange zest and stir until the ingredients just come together. Add the egg yolks and flour and mix to make a firm dough. The pastry will be even better if you make it in the food processor. Remove the dough from the bowl and wrap tightly in cling film; then chill in the fridge for about 1 hour.

Preheat the oven to 200°C/400°F/Gas Mark 6 and grease patty tins.

Roll out half the dough on a floured surface to a thickness of about 5 mm (¼ inch) and use a cutter to cut out pastry discs which will line the bases of the patty tins. Carefully line the tins with the pastry and then spoon in enough mincemeat to fill no more than three-quarters full.

Brush a little beaten egg around the inside rim of the pastry. Roll out the remaining pastry and cut out smaller circles to make lids for the pies. Place on top of the mincemeat and pinch around the edges to seal. Lightly brush across the lids to glaze and sprinkle over a little brown sugar, then use a sharp knife to make a small hole in the centre.

Bake in the oven for about 12–15 minutes, or until the pastry is golden brown and crisp. Allow the mince pies to cool before removing from the tins.

To enjoy at their best, follow my lead and serve with clotted cream and a glass of brandy!

tangy lime and lavender tart

for the pastry

115 g (4 oz) salted butter

225 g (8 oz) plain white flour

1 large egg, plus ½ eggshell full of water

10 fresh lavender heads (about heaped 20 ml/4 teaspoons)

juice and finely grated zest of 1 large lime

for the sponge

115 g (4 oz) unsalted butter, softened

115 g (4 oz) caster sugar

2 eggs, beaten

115 g (4 oz) self-raising flour

175 g (6 oz) blackcurrant or blueberry jam

for the icing

about 115 g (4 oz) icing sugar, sifted

serves 6–8

As an apprentice, I had to make a Lancaster lemon tart – soft sponge drizzled with lemon icing – for afternoon tea; it was delicious. So I have adapted the recipe to use lime and lavender instead. This, along with Lavender Shortbread (page 293) are two very nice ways of incorporating an unusual culinary ingredient. Moroccan and French cooks still use lavender in their cooking, but only occasionally, and then very cautiously.

In this recipe I use fresh lavender, as dried can taste like old socks, unless you have dried it yourself.

Preheat the oven to 180°C/350°F/Gas Mark 4. To make the pastry, rub the butter into the flour to resemble fine breadcrumbs. Crack in the egg, then add the water and lavender with half the lime juice. Mix lightly together with a fork and then gently knead to make a dough – do not overwork or the pastry will lose shape and blister when cooked.

Use the pastry to line a greased 23 cm (9-inch) diameter, 4 cm (1¾-inch) deep fluted flan tin, do not roll out the pastry too thickly or it will not cook in the same time as the sponge mixture. Trim off the excess pastry and thumb up the edge. Prick the base all over using a fork and chill for about 30 minutes.

To make the sponge, beat the butter and sugar together until pale. Add about a quarter of the egg and beat well using your hand (I believe that the heat of your hand really is beneficial to the mixture as it helps to prevent the mixture from separating). Gradually beat in the rest of the egg and then add the flour and fold in again with your hand. Lightly stir in the lime zest, being careful not to overwork the mixture.

Spread the jam evenly over the base of the chilled pastry case and then spoon the sponge mixture on top. Spread out evenly, place on a baking sheet (the added heat from the tray helps the pastry to cook the bottom of the tart) and cook in the oven for about 25 minutes or until the sponge is well risen, nicely brown and firm to the touch – if the sponge begins to come away from the sides it is starting to overcook. Allow to cool on a cooling rack.

Prick the cooled sponge all over with a skewer. Gradually mix enough icing sugar into the remaining lime juice to make a soft icing, then spread evenly over the sponge and leave to set. Serve in thick slices, with double cream.

FRITTERS
& FRIED
PUDDINGS

British cooks have always fried things. Fritters have been made here for centuries. Elizabethan cooks were probably the first to cook fruit fritters using apples, cherries and quinces. They viewed all raw fruit with great suspicion, cooking some apple and quince dishes for as long as six hours.

Like every other part of cooking deep-frying is a great skill; it takes time to learn. Oils, cooking temperature, coatings, draining, all play a vital role in getting the end product absolutely perfect.

The first rule is that new oil must be heated to a temperature of 185°C and cooled, and then re-heated. This process I call proving. It makes sure that the oil will brown the food slightly and the food will taste better. New oil cooks without colouring, so people overcook the food because they cannot see any colour. Sounds bizarre, but it's true.

The second rule is to cut whatever you're cooking into smallish pieces. Not only do they cook quicker, they also cook more evenly.

Third rule: make sure the temperature of the oil is spot on. The batter or coating has to seal straight away, otherwise the oil will seep into the food and spoil it. Don't overload the fryer, as this can cause the temperature of the oil to drop by as much as 20°C. Cook a little at a time.

Fourth rule: get the consistency of the batter right. Too thin and it will fall away in the hot oil and expose the food. (Remember the batter or coating is there to protect the food from the hot oil.) Too thick and you end up with a leaden stodge, similar to cheap sweet and sour pork balls.

Fifth and final rule: never fill the pan more than one-third full with oil. This ensures that the oil doesn't rise over the rim of the pan when the food is added.

For me there are really only two ways to make a batter. The first is a Japanese tempura-style batter made with egg whites and cornflour, great for vegetables and fish. The other is a great all-round batter which I use all the time. I make it with lager or sparkling water, self-raising flour and a touch of flavouring. Just remember not to overwork the flour when adding the liquid as this makes the batter very heavy and leaden. Make the batter at the last moment to ensure a light, crisp, airy result.

In this section I cook a few great favourites of mine. One is deep-fried custard. I know what you are thinking, but, believe you me, it is delicious and only takes a few minutes to cook. This is not really a new idea; Elizabethan cooks would make curd fritters, flavouring and colouring them with marigold petals or saffron. Two other fried favourites are doughnuts and five-spice fritters made with choux paste. I cooked doughnuts for a whole week perfecting the recipe (my next-door neighbour is sick of the sight of them). The five-spice fritters are delicious with a cup of strong coffee and a brandy.

see also

sautéed apples in calvados *page 212*
sautéed bananas with brown sugar, lime and cream *page 213*

pineapple fritters
with hot bitter chocolate sauce

1 baby pineapple, 'Del Monte' variety
if possible
2.5 ml (½ teaspoon) finely grated
lemon zest
2.5 ml (½ teaspoon) lemongrass powder
45 ml (3 tablespoons) dark rum

for the sauce
85 g (3 oz) good-quality cocoa powder
175 g (6 oz) castor sugar
40 g (1½ oz) cold unsalted butter, cubed

for the batter
225 g (8 oz) self-raising flour
about 425 ml (¾ pint) sparkling
mineral water
2.5 ml (½ teaspoon) ground allspice
vegetable oil, for deep-frying
castor sugar and ground allspice,
to decorate

serves 4–6

Pineapple is one of my favourite fruit; it's very refreshing and versatile and good value for money. The best way to tell if a pineapple is ripe is to make sure it has a wonderful deep aroma – I don't think the method of checking ripeness by puling out the leaves is as reliable. The pineapple should have a golden colour and not be green and hard.

Deep-frying is a great way of preparing this gorgeous fruit, especially with a wicked bitter chocolate sauce. If you want to go the whole hog, a big scoop of vanilla ice cream to finish it off is pure decadence.

Remove the top from the pineapple with a sharp knife and then cut off the bottom as well. Carefully cut down the sides to remove the skin, taking care not to remove too much flesh. Lay the fruit on its side and cut into 1 cm (½-inch) slices; then cut each slice into six wedges, leaving the core in. Place the pineapple wedges in a bowl and sprinkle over the lemon zest, lemongrass powder and dark rum. Leave to marinate for 1 hour.

Meanwhile, make the chocolate sauce. Bring 300 ml (½ pint) of cold water, the cocoa powder and sugar to the boil in a pan. Simmer for 2 minutes and then take off the heat and whisk in the butter until melted. Strain through a sieve and keep warm.

Finally, make the batter. Sift the flour into a large bowl and then whisk in enough fizzy water to make a thick batter (about the same consistency as Yorkshire pudding batter). Mix in the allspice and allow to stand for 5 minutes.

Fill a deep-fryer or a deep pan one-third full with oil and heat to 180°C. Pat dry the pineapple on kitchen paper and then dip in the batter to coat. Cooking in batches, drop the pineapple carefully into the hot oil and cook until golden and crisp. Drain well on kitchen paper and sprinkle with castor sugar and allspice.

Pour a pool of hot chocolate sauce into shallow bowls and arrange a few fritters on top. Serve immediately, with ice cream if you like.

doughnuts

50 ml (2 fl oz) whole milk

200 g (7 oz) strong white bread flour, sifted

100 g (3½ oz) plain white flour

7g sachet fast-acting dried yeast

40 g (1½ oz) unrefined castor sugar

3 pinches of salt

1 large egg, beaten

35 g (1¼ oz) unsalted butter, melted

vegetable oil, for deep-frying

unrefined icing sugar and ground cinnamon, to decorate

makes

about 25 small doughnuts

These, as we all know, are delicious. Doughnuts can be stuffed with raspberry jam and rolled in sugar but I prefer them rolled in unrefined icing sugar for a nice caramel edge, and cinnamon.

I think the secret of a feather-light doughnut is the mixture of bread and soft flours, and very slightly 'over-proving' the dough: when they are double in size, leave them for a further 10 minutes and then pop them into the hot fat four or five at a time, they will puff up straight away. I use a wok half-filled with sunflower oil with a sugar thermometer or a free-standing fryer fitted with a thermostat.

Warm the milk and 100 ml (3½ fl oz) of cold water together to blood temperature. Mix both the flours with the yeast, sugar, salt and egg.

Add the melted butter to the flour mixture and then add about half the warm milk and water – as strong flours vary greatly in absorption capacity you might not need all the liquid. Mix to a dough, adding a little more liquid at a time if necessary. The mixture must be very soft and pliable but not too sticky. Tip on to a lightly floured work surface and knead lightly; then return to the bowl, cover with cling film and leave in a warm place to prove for 30 minutes or until doubled in size.

When fully risen, remove the cling film (there will be a sweet, warm smell) and gently knead on a lightly floured surface to 'knock back'. The dough will be very soft but not sticky. Mould into small balls the size of a small apricot (remember they will rise substantially). Place on an oiled baking sheet, cover with cling film and then prove again for 20–30 minutes or until almost doubled in size.

Heat the oil in a deep-fryer until the temperature reaches 190°C. Drop three or four doughnuts into the hot oil and cook for about 2 minutes or until nicely browned; then flip over and cook for a further 3 minutes. Remove from the hot oil and drain on kitchen paper. Repeat the process, making sure the oil comes back to the right temperature each time.

Sprinkle the cooked doughnuts with unrefined icing sugar and ground cinnamon and eat warm.

deep-fried apple turnovers
with Crunchie ice cream

5 Granny Smith apples

grated zest and juice of 1 lemon

grated zest and juice of 1 orange

4 filo pastry sheets, measuring about
29 × 23 cm (11½ × 9 inches)

1 egg, beaten

icing sugar, to decorate

for the ice cream

400 g (14 oz) good-quality vanilla
ice cream

4 Crunchie bars, chopped

serves 4

The great thing about this pudding is the combination of hot and cold textures and flavours. Just make sure you dry out the apple purée well or the turnovers will end up soggy.

Peel, core and chop the apples into small pieces and then place in a heavy-bottomed pan. Add the zest and juice from both the lemon and orange. Cook for about 35–40 minutes or until soft and dry. Place in a sieve and leave overnight if possible to drain and dry further – you should end up with a dry, tight stew.

Cut one of the filo sheets in half lengthways. Lightly brush beaten egg over the top half of each piece and then fold up the bottom halves so they are on top. Place a small spoonful of the apple mixture in one corner, brush egg along the edges and then fold in half on the diagonal and seal well. Repeat to make eight turnovers.

Take the ice cream out of the freezer and allow to soften slightly. Fold in the Crunchie pieces and re-freeze.

Deep-fry the turnovers in batches in hot oil (170°C) for 3–4 minutes or until golden brown and crisp. Drain on kitchen paper and then dust with icing sugar.

Serve the hot fritters with the ice cream.

custard brioches

2 large all-butter brioche buns, about 9 cm
(3½ inches) diameter and 7.5 cm
(3 inches) deep

2 large eggs

100 ml (3½ fl oz) double cream

50 ml (2 fl oz) whole milk

55 g (2 oz) soft light brown sugar

2.5 ml (½ teaspoon) vanilla extract

serves 4

This is one of my favourites, a gorgeous creamy dessert that most people find hard to resist and it is very simple indeed. The secret of this dish is to make sure you cook the brioches very slowly so the outside is set and just browned and the inside soft and jelly-like, just set.

My favourite ice cream to serve with this is Caramel Pecan (page 176) but vanilla is also very good – the combination of hot and cold is amazing.

Place the brioches on a chopping board, slice about 1 cm (½ inch) off the bottom and then cut them in half horizontally.

Mix together the eggs, cream, milk, sugar and vanilla thoroughly. Sit the brioche, cut-side down, in a shallow dish, making sure they sit nice and tightly together. Pour over the egg mixture and leave to soak for the best part of 1 hour (or overnight in a fridge is better), carefully turning occasionally. As they soak up the mixture the brioche will become heavy and soggy.

Preheat the oven to 160°C/325°F/Gas Mark 3. The secret to cooking the brioches is to cook them in a completely dry, un-oiled pan. Just warm up an ovenproof frying pan on the hob and then pop in the brioches, cut-side down, and gently cook for a few minutes until the bottoms are slightly brown and set. Turn the brioche over, pop the pan into the oven and bake for about 15–20 minutes or until they are just cooked, so you end up with a soft, but set centre. Remove and keep warm.

Serve with a ball of ice cream on top of each brioche half.

deep-fried custard
with honey and lemon

300 ml (½ pint) whole milk

25 g (1 oz) Bird's custard powder

35 g (1¼ oz) castor sugar

30 ml (2 tablespoons) plain white flour

3 eggs, beaten

100 g (3½ oz) ground almonds

100 g (3½ oz) dry, fine breadcrumbs

vegetable oil, for deep-frying

castor sugar, to decorate

for the sauce

60 ml (4 tablespoons) honey

finely grated zest and juice of 1 large lemon

serves 4–6

This idea sounds a little bizarre, but is incredibly tasty. The secret is to cook the finished custards very quickly indeed, then leave them to warm through so you end up with a crisp, golden, nutty outside and warm melting inside. The honey and lemon are a powerful flavouring drizzled over at the last moment.

Lightly oil a 22 cm (8½-inch) square dish or tin (a tin roughly this size will ensure you get the right thickness of custard, about 3–5 mm/⅛–¼ inch).

Pour three-quarters of the milk into a pan and bring to the boil. Add the rest of the milk to the custard powder and mix until incorporated, then add the sugar. When the milk is boiling, pour on to the custard mixture and whisk well. Return to the pan and bring back to the boil, stirring all the time. When thickened and boiling, remove from the heat and pour into the oiled dish. Spread out evenly, leave to cool, then cover and chill for 2 hours.

Meanwhile, make the sauce. Heat the honey and lemon zest and juice together in a small pan and cook for a minute or two to thicken slightly, then cool and set aside until needed.

When you're ready to fry the custard fritters, put the flour on to a plate, pour the eggs into a bowl and place the almonds and breadcrumbs in two separate bowls.

Turn the chilled, set custard out on to a chopping board and carefully cut into 4 × 2 cm (1½ × ¾-inch) pieces. Lift one piece at a time using a palette knife and dust in flour, then dip in the egg. Cover with a layer of almonds, dip back into the egg and finally coat in breadcrumbs. Do make sure you seal the custards well in the coatings or they will fall apart in the hot oil! Keep cool while you coat the rest of the custard pieces.

Heat the vegetable oil in a deep-fat fryer, or use a deep pan filled one-third full with oil, until the temperature reaches 195°C (remember, never fill a pan more than one-third full with oil).

Cook the custards in the hot fat, no more than four at a time, for 30 seconds to 1 minute; they should look crisp and golden and the inside should be just warm.

Drain on kitchen paper, and keep warm for a minute or so, then sprinkle over a little castor sugar. Cook the remaining custards in small batches, making sure the oil reaches 195°C before each batch of cooking.

Place the custards on serving plates and drizzle over a little of the honey and lemon sauce. I also like to serve a ball of vanilla ice cream on the side.

CHOCOLATE
DESSERTS
& CAKES

No puddings book could be written without including chocolate. In Britain we consume about 11 kg per person per year, making us serious chocoholics. It is probably the most important ingredient for puddings and desserts, apart from sugar.

Over the years I have really enjoyed cooking with chocolate – and I still do. I find it such a satisfying ingredient because you always, and I mean always, end up with something spectacular for your guests. It might be a rich-tasting mousse with coffee sauce, a visually stunning Easter egg wrapped up in ribbon, or a professional-looking hot bitter chocolate and chilli soufflé. You simply cannot go wrong.

Chocolate has come a very

long way since it began to be cultivated in South America around 500 BC. It wasn't until Christopher Columbus was given some beans in 1502 that anybody had really seen cacao beans in the northern hemisphere. The Spanish brought the beans back home about 30 years later; they then kept the whole chocolate thing a secret for the best part of 40 years.

The chocolate we eat everyday really isn't chocolate at all, as the amount of cocoa solids is very small indeed. The cocoa solids are mixed with milk powder, vegetable fat and sugar to end up with the creamy confection we all love. The rest of Europe's thoughts on our chocolate are well documented: they detest it.

Couverture is a different thing altogether; it contains a much higher percentage of cocoa solids. The cocoa solids are mixed with sugar and formed into large blocks. We chefs use couverture for desserts because it is chocolate in its purest form. It has a very deep, slightly bitter flavour and a smooth, velvety feel on the tongue and mouth.

I have tried to give a cross-section of chocolate recipes, from the ever-popular chocolate tart and chocolate pudding to simple frozen chocolate torte and roulade. All will, I hope, inspire you and, as I said earlier, you'll never fail to impress.

techniques

I recommend you use chocolate with the highest percentage of cocoa solids you can buy (you hear chefs say this all the time). Most supermarkets or delis now stock dark bitter chocolate with about 70 per cent solids and I believe now you can also buy a chocolate with an incredible 90 per cent cocoa solids, although I have not cooked with it.

When it comes to cooking with chocolate the rules are very simple: do not overheat the chocolate or it will thicken and turn lumpy. If this happens it's best to throw it away and start again. Probably the most important rule is to remember that the slightest drop of water or condensed steam will thicken and ruin chocolate very quickly indeed. Again, the only thing to do is to throw it away and start again, so be careful.

Melting chocolate
Put a pan about half full of water on to heat. Break the chocolate into chunks. Place the chunks in a heatproof bowl and sit the bowl over the pan. Keep the water at a simmer and stir occasionally while the chocolate melts.

Make sure that the simmering water

doesn't touch the bottom of the bowl or that steam from the water doesn't get into the chocolate as either of these can cause the chocolate to 'seize': it becomes thick and grainy and the texture of the finished dish will be spoiled.

Avoid overheating chocolate, which will make it lumpy. Be particularly careful with white chocolate, which is more prone to overheating.

You can melt chocolate in the microwave but use low power and keep checking to see whether it is soft: the chunks hold their shape more than if melted over water and it's easy to think that they aren't ready because they look solid, and thus to overheat them.

If you're adding alcohol or orange juice to flavour the chocolate, it's best not to do this until the chocolate has melted.

see also

steamed hot chocolate pudding
with chocolate fudge sauce

3 large eggs

125 g (4½ oz) castor sugar

100 g (3½ oz) plain white flour, sifted

25 g (1 oz) cocoa powder, sifted

100 g (3½ oz) unsalted butter, melted

125 g (4½ oz) bitter chocolate,

70% minimum cocoa solids,

finely chopped

for the sauce

85 g (3 oz) unsalted butter

140 g (5 oz) soft brown sugar

300 ml (½ pint) double cream

85 g (3 oz) bitter chocolate,

70% minimum cocoa solids,

chopped

serves 6–8

This pudding can be made the day before if kept chilled; next day, cut into portions and reheat in the microwave for 2–3 minutes on full power; take care it doesn't burn.

Well butter a 2-litre (3½-pint) heatproof bowl and a piece of foil (big enough to cover the dish).

Place the eggs and castor sugar in the mixing bowl of a food mixer and whisk on a high speed for 15 minutes or until very thick and foamy (see page 276). When ready, remove the bowl from the machine and carefully fold in the flour and cocoa powder – take care not to over mix or the sponge will be tough and leaden. Next, add the melted butter and chopped chocolate, again folding in carefully.

Spoon the mixture into the prepared bowl, cover with the buttered foil and cook in a steamer for about 1 hour, or until cooked – the sponge will be very soft and spongy. Do not overcook or the sponge will be leaden.

Meanwhile, make the sauce. Heat the butter and sugar together in a pan until melted, stirring occasionally. Add the cream and chocolate and bring to the boil, stirring all the time so the sauce does not stick. When completely melted, you can pass the sauce through a fine sieve if you like. Cover the sauce with cling film and keep warm.

Turn the pudding out while it's still warm and pour over plenty of the sauce. A nice spoon of double cream over the pudding is completely over the top but absolutely gorgeous.

bitter chocolate tart

150 g (5½ oz) bitter chocolate, 70% minimum cocoa solids

150 g (5½ oz) milk chocolate

2 large eggs, plus 2 large egg yolks, at room temperature

60 g (2¼ oz) castor sugar

150 g (5½ oz) unsalted butter, melted

23 × 3 cm (9- × 1½-inch) sweet shortcrust or cocoa pastry case, baked blind (page 40 or 41)

icing sugar, to decorate

Coffee Bean Syrup, to serve (page 230)

serves 6–8

The secret here is to not refrigerate the tart, it must be eaten at room temperature once cooled. If you have to chill it, make sure you take it out of the fridge at least an hour before eating. For a real chocolate-addict's version, use chocolate-flavoured pastry for the flan case.

Preheat the oven to 220°C/425°F/Gas Mark 7. Melt the two chocolates together in a heatproof bowl over a pan of gently simmering water (see page 81).

Place the eggs, yolks and sugar in the bowl of a food mixer and whisk at high speed until very thick (see page 276). Remove the bowl from the machine and carefully stir in the melted chocolate, taking care not to knock too much air out from the eggs. Finally, fold in the melted butter, again very carefully.

Place the baked-blind flan case on a baking sheet, pour the chocolate mixture into the pastry shell and cook in the oven for 7–8 minutes or until just set – do not let the edges of the tart soufflé up. Remove from the oven and leave to cool on a wire rack.

Eat at room temperature, cut into wedges, dusted heavily with icing sugar and with a little fresh coffee syrup. I also like to serve a little clotted cream, but that is entirely optional.

white chocolate mousse
with coffee syrup

250 g (9 oz) good-quality white chocolate

2 large eggs, plus 2 large egg yolks

2 gelatine leaves, soaked in cold water

375 ml (13 fl oz) double cream,
lightly whipped

15 ml (1 tablespoon) white rum

Coffee Bean Syrup (page 230), to serve

serves 6

We often see bitter chocolate mousse so it's nice to ring the changes. White chocolate isn't actually chocolate at all, it contains cocoa butter rather than cocoa solids, and is normally packed with milk powder and extra sugar. Some brands use vegetable oil as well, so check when buying. Take care when melting white chocolate as it has a tendency to thicken for no reason at all.

Melt the white chocolate in a heatproof bowl over a pan of gently simmering water (see page 81).

Whisk the eggs and yolks in a heatproof bowl over another pan of gently simmering water, until thick and hot. Add the softened gelatine and whisk until dissolved. Then remove from the heat and continue whisking to cool. For a lighter mousse, add half a leaf of gelatine and set in glasses rather than moulds (see page 99).

This is the tricky part – pour the chocolate into the eggs and whisk well, the mixture will thicken and start to look strange but don't worry. Straight away add half the cream and whisk well.

When fully incorporated, finally add the rest of the whipped cream and the rum, and carefully fold in. Pour into six very lightly oiled 150 ml (¼-pint) pudding moulds and chill well, overnight if possible.

To serve, dip the moulds into hot water, then turn the mousses out and surround with coffee syrup. Decorate with a few of the beans from the syrup. It's also nice to serve 'cigarette' biscuits with this mousse.

iced glazed chocolate torte

for the sponge

3 eggs

100 g (3½ oz) unrefined castor sugar

90 g (3¼ oz) plain white flour, sifted

10 g (¼ oz) good-quality cocoa powder, sifted

chocolate liqueur or brandy

for the filling

double-quantity of basic meringue (page 130)

275 g (9½ oz) good-quality bitter chocolate, melted but not too hot (see page 81)

200 ml (7 fl oz) double cream, lightly whipped

for the glaze

2½ gelatine leaves

85 g (3 oz) good-quality cocoa powder

85 g (3 oz) unrefined castor sugar

25 g (1 oz) unsalted butter

Serves 6–8

As an apprentice, I had to make torten all the time. In those days they were all filled and decorated with butter cream, these have, sadly, become a bit unfashionable. So, with this in mind, I have crossed a parfait with a torte and ended up with a very rich and scrummy dessert.

It can be made well in advance, and defrosted until just soft enough to cut, then glazed with a bitter chocolate sauce to cut the richness. It should be eaten like an Italian *semifreddo* (a semi-frozen mousse).

Preheat the oven to 180°C/350°F/Gas Mark 4. Grease and base-line a 25 cm diameter × 6 cm deep (10 × 2½ inch) spring-form cake tin.

To make the sponge, whisk the eggs and sugar together, preferably in a food mixer, and whisk at a medium speed until they are very thick and holding their own weight (see page 276). Carefully fold in the sifted flour and cocoa and mix well. Spoon into the greased cake tin. Place in the oven and cook for about 20 minutes, or until well risen and springy to the touch.

When cooked, cool slightly, run a knife around the edge to release, then open the tin. Cool.

Remove the sponge from the bottom of the tin and wash the tin well. Re-assemble the tin and line with cling film. Invert the sponge and replace in the lined tin (it should come just under halfway up). Sprinkle with chocolate liqueur or brandy.

To make the filling, make the meringue and whisk until very stiff. Fold in the melted chocolate carefully and finally add the cream and mix well, but do not over mix. Spoon into the tin and cover with cling film. Freeze overnight.

To make the glaze, put the gelatine leaves to soak in cold water (see page 99). Place all the other ingredients, except the gelatine, in a small pan

with 275 ml (9½ fl oz) of cold water and heat gently to dissolve the sugar. Increase the heat and bring to the boil and then simmer for 20 seconds, stirring all the time. Remove from the heat and stir in the softened gelatine. Cool until at setting point.

Meanwhile, remove the torte from the freezer, undo the outside ring and carefully lift out of the mould, peel off the cling film and place on a wire rack with a tray underneath so it's ready for the glaze to go on as soon as the glaze begins to set.

Quickly pour over the setting glaze and spread over the torte, taking care to cover the whole thing including the sides; the glaze will set very quickly. Chill again for 20 minutes.

Carefully place on a large plate and cut into large wedges. Serve with pouring cream.

bitter chocolate mousse

2 large eggs, plus 2 large egg yolks

350 g (12 oz) extra-bitter chocolate, broken

into small pieces and melted (see page 81)

550 ml (19 fl oz) whipping cream,

lightly whipped

50 ml (2 fl oz) dark rum

to serve

Fresh Coffee Sauce (page 242)

double cream, lightly whipped

serves 6–8

This recipe came from a very talented chef, Allan Garth, who gave me a job at Gravetye Manor in 1985. I think the only reason he took me on was that I had just left the Lake District, where he had been brought up. He always ribbed me about 'the scruffy letter' I had written to him asking for a job! In the end I spent, on and off, the best part of four years there, which was probably the happiest time I had as a young chef, learning the art of being a pastry chef.

This mousse is very rich and dense and the only way to eat it is in large scoops similar to eating ice cream, with lightly whipped double cream and fresh coffee sauce.

Just make it and let it set in a large bowl, it's not be mucked about with!

Whisk the eggs and egg yolks in a heatproof bowl over a pan of gently simmering water, until thick and cooked; this will take about 15 minutes – I find the best thing to use is an electric hand whisk. Take care the eggs do not overcook or scramble. Remove the bowl from the pan and whisk for a couple of minutes to cool slightly.

This is the important stage: pour the whisked egg mixture into the hot melted chocolate and whisk well and very quickly: you can be quite brutal here. The mixture will look as though it is starting to separate but persevere. When halfway incorporated, add half the cream, and quickly whisk well. The reason you have to move a bit sharpish here is that the temperature of the cold cream can set the chocolate and egg very quickly indeed, but you should end up with a very smooth texture. Panic over, finally whisk in the rest of the cream and add the rum. Pour into a bowl, cover and chill overnight.

Using a hot spoon, scrape off large curls of mousse and serve in glasses, pouring over a little fresh coffee sauce and double cream.

passion-fruit mousse
with passion-fruit jelly and glazed bananas

for the mousse

250 ml (9 fl oz) whole milk

4 egg yolks

70 g (2½ oz) castor sugar

2 gelatine leaves, soaked in cold water

10 passion-fruit

300 ml (½ pint) whipping cream,
lightly whipped

for the jelly

juice and seeds from 5 passion-fruit

25 g (1 oz) castor sugar

1 gelatine leaf, soaked in cold water
(see page 99)

for the bananas

3 ripe bananas

castor sugar, to taste

serves 6

This is a very light mousse set in a glass or bowl. It has something of an old-fashioned syllabub consistency, so you cannot turn it out successfully – the idea is to get a fresh, light, mousse packed with flavour. Passion-fruit are ideal, this small fruit does not yield too much juice but, boy, does it pack a punch! Make sure every last seed and drop of juice is removed from the skins. If you want to be really posh, make the jelly as suggested below, pour on to the top of the chilled mousse and set again

I found that the more wrinkled (ripe) the fruits, the more juice you seem to get, also the fruit seems a little sweeter, but these are just my thoughts. I really love this fruit; whether in a hot soufflé in their own shells (page 120), a frozen mousse or a sorbet, passion-fruit have such a unique flavour.

To make the mousse, bring the milk to the boil. Meanwhile, whisk the egg yolks and sugar together for about 2 minutes until slightly pale. Pour the boiling milk over the egg and sugar mixture, stir well and pour back into the pan. Cook over a low heat, stirring continuously, until the custard thickens and lightly coats the back of a wooden spoon.

Remove the custard from the heat, add the gelatine and stir until dissolved, then strain into a clean bowl and allow to cool.

Meanwhile, cut the passion-fruit in half and scoop out the flesh using a teaspoon (make sure you get every last seed). Blitz in a food processor or using a hand blender until all the flesh and juice has been removed from the seeds. Take care not to break up the seeds too much or you will end up with tiny black dots in the finished mousse – I find it best to 'pulse' the machine.

Push all the juice through a fine sieve using a large spoon. Measure the juice: you should end up with 200 ml (7 fl oz); if slightly under just top up with a little fresh orange juice.

At this point, remove the whipped cream from the fridge if necessary and leave at room temperature for 10 minutes to take the chill off it, this will ensure the mousse doesn't set too quickly, allowing you to spoon into wine glasses.

Either place the custard in the fridge, stirring occasionally or carefully sit it in a bowl of iced water and stir constantly until the mixture is at setting point and is starting to thicken – take care the custard really is at setting point or the finished mousse will separate. Add the passion-fruit juice and stir carefully. Finally, add the whipped cream and stir until fully incorporated, you may have to speed up at this point so the mousse does not set on you. Immediately spoon into glasses and chill well.

Meanwhile, make the jelly – blitz the passion-fruit seeds and juice together as before and then pass through a fine sieve, discarding the seeds.

Gently heat the sugar and 100 ml (3½ fl oz) of cold water together to dissolve, then remove from the heat and cool slightly. Stir in the softened gelatine until dissolved and allow to cool.

Once cool, add the passion-fruit juice (not adding the juice until this point ensures that the finished jelly has the freshest possible taste). Pass through a fine sieve or piece of muslin into a jug, and then pour a thin layer over the chilled mousses and chill for 20 minutes, or until set.

The glazed bananas are very simple to do – peel the bananas and slice at an angle, place on a non-stick baking sheet and sprinkle with a little castor sugar. Glaze with a blowtorch (see page 39) or place under a hot grill. Repeat the process (this is the secret to even glazing) and then leave to cool.

Stand the mousses on plates, surrounded by slices of glazed banana.

strawberry mousse

280 g (10 oz) ripe English strawberries

2 gelatine leaves, soaked in cold water

2 large eggs plus 2 large egg yolks

175 g (6 oz) castor sugar

150 ml (¼ pint) double cream,
very lightly whipped

Raspberry Sauce and Meringue 'Asparagus'
(pages 246 and 134), to serve

serves 4–6

We used to make this recipe all the time in the early eighties. The eggs are uncooked, so do take care to whom you serve this. It's the best flavoured mousse I know and also the simplest: the secret is to get the mousse at the right setting point, without knocking out too much air.

This recipe can be used for all summer fruits – blackberry is my other favourite.

First, make the strawberry purée: liquidise the strawberries and then pass through a fine sieve to remove the seeds. You may need to add a touch of water, say 1 tablespoon, to get the whole thing going but do not dilute the purée more than absolutely necessary.

Remove the gelatine from the water, shake off any excess, place in a small pan and gently heat until melted (see page 99).

Whisk the eggs and yolks with the castor sugar until the mixture is very thick and foamy and holding its own weight (see page 276).

Add the melted gelatine to the egg and sugar mixture and stir through very carefully. Carefully stir in the strawberry purée – do not over mix or all the air you have put in via the whisking process will be lost and you will end up with a heavy, dull mousse.

Finally, add the lightly whipped cream; the mousse should start to thicken quite quickly now but, especially in the summer months, you may need to sit the bowl over a larger bowl of iced water at this point and stir the mixture to encourage the setting process. Just as the mixture is beginning to set and hold its own weight, pour into a large mould or individual glasses and chill until set.

Serve with raspberry sauce and meringue 'asparagus' spears.

rhubarb tiramisù

425 g (15 oz) new-season rhubarb
175 g (6 oz) granulated sugar
12 sponge fingers
2 large eggs
heaped 45 ml (3 tablespoons) plus heaped
30 ml (2 tablespoons) castor sugar
250 ml (9 fl oz) double cream
350 g (12 oz) mascarpone cheese
cocoa powder, to decorate

serves 4–6

Over the past few years Italian food has become one of the most popular types of food in Britain. There is scarcely a restaurant in the land that does not feature pasta, plum tomatoes or balsamic vinegar somewhere on its menu. The trouble is that most of it is complete rubbish. Throwing a handful of sea salt and too much balsamic vinegar over a bowl of underripe and tasteless winter tomatoes doesn't make them Italian. The same can be said of puddings. I love pannacotta – a sort of Italian blancmange – but it never seems to be done well.

Tiramisù is the best Italian sweet by far, a perfect combination of cream, mascarpone and coffee. I have spent a long time trying to get it right and I think that you will enjoy this rhubarb version. The combination seems to work really well and is a great way to end a heavy meal. Oh, and by the way, we actually got rhubarb from the Italians in the eighteenth century.

Wash the rhubarb well in plenty of cold water and then cut into 1 cm (½-inch) cubes. Pop into a pan with the granulated sugar and 225 ml (8 fl oz) of cold water and gently bring to the boil. As soon as the liquid starts to boil, remove from the heat and carefully place a piece of greaseproof paper directly on top of the syrup and rhubarb. Leave to cool for at least 5–6 hours.

When the rhubarb is cooled, carefully strain into a colander, keeping all the gorgeous pinkish syrup.

Arrange the sponge fingers in a suitable dish or glass bowl, I use a dish that measures about 28 × 23 × 5 cm deep (11 × 9 × 2 inches). Spoon over about half of the rhubarb syrup and leave to soak in – within about 15 minutes most of the syrup will have disappeared. You can add a little more syrup if you want to, it's up to you but I prefer it not to be too soggy. Chill well.

Next place the eggs and heaped 45 ml (3 tablespoons) of castor sugar in a heatproof bowl and gently whisk over a pan of simmering water until they are thick and creamy and cooked; this will take a few minutes. Pop into a mixer and whisk at high speed until thick and cool.

In a separate bowl, whip the double cream until it just makes peaks, do take care as double cream over whips very quickly. Keep at room temperature. Finally – you need plenty of bowls for this pudding! – whisk the mascarpone and heaped 30 ml (2 tablespoons) of castor sugar together until loose and creamy.

Next is the easy bit, I promise! Fold together the mascarpone and double cream, and then carefully fold in the egg mixture to lighten the whole thing. Remove the dish with the soaked sponge fingers from the fridge and sprinkle the poached rhubarb evenly over the top. Spoon over the egg and cream mixture, flatten out with a palette knife and chill well. That's it, dust with cocoa powder and serve with a strong cup of coffee.

caramel mousse

250 g (9 oz) granulated sugar

5 large eggs, plus 2 large egg yolks

25 g (1 oz) castor sugar

4½ gelatine leaves, soaked in cold water

300 ml (½ pint) whipping cream, lightly whipped

finely grated zest of 1 small lemon

serves 6–8

I have cooked this mousse for many years. It's very light and is a perfect way to end a rich, heavy meal. A few strawberries and Rich Lemon Curd Ice Cream (page 175) are just the perfect accompaniment.

Place the granulated sugar in a thick-bottomed saucepan and cook gently until you have a nice dark caramel (see page 171). Carefully add 150 ml (¼ pint) of cold water – don't worry about the noise and spitting, just stand back and be careful. Immediately remove the pan from the heat and pour the contents into a bowl to cool.

Whisk the eggs, yolks and castor sugar together in a large heatproof bowl over a pan of gently simmering water until thick and foamy (see page 276). Remove from the heat, then very carefully sit the bowl of egg froth mixture over a bowl of iced water and stir until cool. Add the cool caramel syrup and fold in carefully.

Lift the leaves of gelatine out of the water and shake off any excess water. Place in a small pan and gently heat to melt the gelatine (see page 99) and then stir into the cooling egg and caramel mixture.

When completely cool, add the whipped cream and lemon zest and continue to stir until the mixture thickens; at this point very quickly pour the mousse mixture into tall glasses or a nice mousse mould before it sets. The mould will need to be wetted or very lightly oiled. Chill for about 4 hours and then invert on to a serving plate and carefully turn out, if you have set the mousse in a mould.

new york style cheesecake

225 (8 oz) sweet shortcrust pastry
(see page 40), or ready-rolled
shortcrust pastry
700 g (1 lb 9 oz) full-fat cream cheese
350 g (12 oz) castor sugar
45 ml (3 tablespoons) vanilla extract
45 ml (3 tablespoons) dark rum
3 pinches of salt
284 ml carton of sour cream
grated zest and juice of 2 large lemons
3 medium eggs, at room temperature,
separated
a pinch of cream of tartar
icing sugar, to decorate

serves 8–10

I didn't like the flavour or the texture of this type of cheesecake when I first tasted it but, after numerous trips to the States, it has rather grown on me. I was put off by the heavy, cloying texture and rather bland taste. In this recipe I have tried to sort out these problems by lightening the mixture considerably and by adding rum, vanilla and plenty of lemon.

Preheat the oven to 190°C/375°F/Gas Mark 5. Take a 24 cm × 7 cm deep (9 × 3 cm) springform cake tin and grease the base well.

Roll out the pastry or, if using ready-rolled pastry, lay it on a lightly floured board or work surface.

Place the tin on top and carefully cut around the base. Lift off the tin, carefully place the pastry inside the tin and press to the edges.

Prick well with a fork and cook in the preheated oven for 20 minutes, to set and very lightly brown. Turn the oven down to 160°C/325°F/Gas Mark 3.

Remove the cake tin from the oven and leave to cool. Then grease the inside of the tin.

Beat the cream cheese, sugar, vanilla, rum and salt together until thick and creamy; this will take about 5 minutes in a food mixer. You can use a wooden spoon and beat it by hand, but this will take a little longer.

Add the sour cream, lemon zest and egg yolks and beat well.

Place the egg whites and cream of tartar in a separate bowl and whisk until the whisked whites will just hold their own weight, ribbon fashion; do not over whisk (see page 129).

Place the whites and lemon juice in the cheese mixture and fold in with a large spoon. Pour the mixture into the lined baking tray and smooth out.

Bake in the preheated oven for 45–55 minutes until just set. The outside will soufflé very slightly and the inside will be very slightly runny but this is fine: once cooled and chilled, the cheesecake will set perfectly. The top of

the cheesecake may also crack slightly when cooling but don't worry, this is quite normal.

Once chilled, dust heavily with icing sugar and cut into large wedges. This is nice with Rich Lemon Curd Ice Cream (see page 175) and a little blackcurrant sauce (page 48).

HOT & COLD
SOUFFLÉS

I think that the soufflé must have been invented by mistake. I cannot see anybody thinking of making a soufflé. My theory is this: years ago a chef or cook must have accidentally left an egg tart (very popular with medieval cooks) or whisked sponge too long in the oven. The result was probably a very sorry-looking, split, burnt thing — but well risen, which sparked a thought in the cook's mind.

There really is no secret to a good soufflé. The process is a very simple one, in which minute bubbles of air are trapped and subjected to high heat so that they expand with a little steam – and, hey presto!, a well risen soufflé. Soufflés are very easy to make provided you follow the recipe carefully, but they are also very easy to get wrong. I remember once cooking 120 banana soufflés for a very important New Year's Eve dinner. The pastry chef at the time had everything ready, but neglected to whisk the meringue to the correct consistency. The weight of the banana and pastry cream caused the meringue to collapse and we ended up with risen soufflés that fell over the edge of the dish! Needless to say it was me who had to change my jacket and enter the ballroom and explain to the rather merry bunch that we would have to cook them all again. Since then I have never trusted anybody when it comes to soufflés.

I have tried to give a good variety of soufflés in this chapter, from the old-fashioned pudding soufflés that were popular in the fifties and sixties, through soufflé pancakes (very trendy in the late sixties), to some very modern soufflés like tamarillo, chocolate and chilli, and passion-fruit in its own shell.

techniques

Soufflés are perfect for the home cook, they are quick, easy and very simple to get together, provided you follow some basic rules.

Use very clean utensils: any speck of grease or yolk will break down the egg white. Always use egg whites at room temperature.

Whisk meringue with a tiniest pinch of cream of tartar on a medium speed. This ensures a soft, malleable meringue, easy to stir into custards and purées. Don't over whisk — it prevents the soufflé from rising, making it heavy and firm.

Grease the dishes carefully. This helps the soufflé rise evenly.

Always check the oven temperature; the finished soufflé must be well risen, nicely coloured and warm in the centre.

passion-fruit soufflé
in the shell

8 passion-fruit

2 large eggs, separated

a pinch of cream of tartar

55 g (2 oz) unrefined castor sugar

55 g (2 oz) unrefined icing sugar, sifted,
plus extra to decorate

serves 2

I need to put the record straight here: this is an idea that I once cooked and which Ainsley Harriott stole and put in one of his books – we have a good laugh about it but, strangely enough, he still can't remember where the idea came from!

It's a nice way to end a heavy meal, with the bonus that all the preparation can be done well in advance.

Preheat the oven to 220°C/425°F/Gas Mark 7. Cut the passion-fruit in half and use a teaspoon to remove as much of the pulp and juice as possible. Keep the empty shells. Using a hand-blender on the slowest setting, whizz the passion-fruit pulp and seeds together until very runny and loose. If you do not have a hand-blender then just break up well with a whisk or fork. Strain well through a fine sieve, take care to get as much juice as possible out of the seeds.

Place the egg yolks in a large bowl, add the passion-fruit juice and mix well.

Whisk the egg whites with the cream of tartar on a medium speed until they are thick and foamy (see page 129). Add the castor sugar and continue to whisk on a medium speed until thick and glossy but do not over whisk – the mixture should be soft and silky. Finally, add the icing sugar and mix well again.

Spoon half the meringue into the egg-yolk-and-passion-fruit mixture and whisk together well by hand. Finally, carefully fold in the rest of the meringue.

Spoon into the passion-fruit shell halves, making sure the mixture stands nice and proud. Sit on a baking sheet or in small patty tins, dust with a little icing sugar and bake for about 8 minutes, or until lightly browned. That's it, simple. Serve straight away.

lime soufflé pancakes

for the pancakes

2 eggs

a pinch of castor sugar

a pinch of salt

100 g (3½ oz) plain white flour, sifted

about 200 ml (7 fl oz) whole milk

25 g (1 oz) cold unsalted butter, melted

vegetable oil, for frying

for the filling

finely grated zest and juice
of 2 large limes

60 g (2¼ oz) castor sugar

heaped 7.5 ml (1½ teaspoons) arrowroot,
soaked in cold water

2 eggs, separated

40 g (1½ oz) unsalted butter,
cut in small cubes

for the sauce

juice of 2 limes

30 ml (2 tablespoons) castor sugar

15 g (½ oz) cold, unsalted butter,
cut in small cubes

icing sugar, to decorate

serves 4

Tony Tobin, a good friend of mine, gave me the idea for this recipe. The good thing about this pudding is it's up to you how much lime you put in so if you like your pancakes really limey, then just add more juice and take away some of the sugar. You can also substitute lemon for lime, or even orange.

First, make the pancakes. Break the eggs into a bowl, add the sugar, salt and flour and whisk well. Add enough milk to make a thin batter and then finally add the melted butter and whisk in. Cover and leave to cool.

Heat a little oil in a frying pan. Spoon in enough batter to cover the bottom and cook over a high heat until nicely browned, then flip over and brown on the other side. Lift out and cool on greaseproof paper. Repeat to make four pancakes slightly thicker than the usual crêpes.

Preheat the oven to 220°C/425°F/Gas Mark 7. To make the filling, place the lime juice, zest and 25 g (1 oz) of the castor sugar in a pan and bring to a gentle simmer. Add the arrowroot and bring to the boil, stirring. Take off the stove, and leave to cool for 3 minutes.

Add the egg yolks and butter and whisk in until melted and thickened. Keep warm.

Whisk the egg whites until they become thick and foamy, but not grainy. Add the remaining 35 g (1¼ oz) of castor sugar and whisk until the whites form soft peaks, but do not over whisk them or they will not expand in the oven (see page 129).

Whisk half the meringue into the warm curd mixture, then carefully fold the remaining whites in with a whisk. Divide the mixture between the four pancakes and fold the pancakes in half to enclose. Place on a non-stick baking sheet and bake for 8–10 minutes, or until well risen and nicely browned.

Meanwhile, make the sauce. Bring the lime juice, 15 ml (1 tablespoon) of cold water and the sugar to a simmer in a pan. Whisk in the cold butter to thicken. This is a very powerful sauce, so you'll only need a small spoonful over each pancake.

Using a fish slice, transfer the pancakes on to warm serving plates, spoon over a little of the syrup and dust with icing sugar. Serve with ice cream.

hot lemon and orange
soufflé pudding

45 ml (3 tablespoons) orange or lemon curd

finely grated zest and juice of 1 large orange

finely grated zest and juice of 2 lemons

140 g (5 oz) castor sugar

15 ml (1 tablespoon) arrowroot, slaked in a little cold water

60 g (2¼ oz) unsalted butter

4 eggs, separated

icing sugar, sifted, to decorate

serves 4

This is a quick and fairly simple pudding. You don't have to worry too much about whether it will rise properly because it only needs to set rather than to rise perfectly. It's nice eaten hot or cold.

Preheat the oven to 200°C/400°F/Gas Mark 6. Spoon the curd into the bottom of a 23 cm (9-inch) diameter × 7.5 cm (3-inch) deep oval baking or soufflé dish and spread out evenly.

Place the orange and lemon juices and zests in a pan with 70 g (2½ oz) of the castor sugar. Bring to a gentle simmer and cook for 1 minute. Stir in the arrowroot to thicken. Whisk in the butter and then remove from the heat. Cool slightly and then mix in the egg yolks. Keep warm.

Whisk the egg whites in a bowl until they are thick and foamy but not grainy. Add 35 g (1¼ oz) of the remaining castor sugar and whisk until they form soft peaks but are not too stiff. Fold in the remaining 35 g (1¼ oz) of castor sugar (see page 129).

Pour the cooked juice and butter mixture into a large mixing bowl, add half the meringue mixture and whisk well. Add the rest of the whites and fold in carefully. Spoon into the baking dish and bake for about 15–20 minutes, or until nicely browned and slightly risen. The secret to this pudding is to make sure that the middle is soft and the outside is nice and brown.

Dust with a little icing sugar and serve with cream.

banana soufflés

250 ml (9 fl oz) whole milk

3 large eggs, separated

120 g (4¼ oz) castor sugar

40 g (1½ oz) plain white flour

2 bananas, finely mashed with a fork

a pinch of cream of tartar

icing sugar, to decorate

serves 4

This soufflé base can be used for all sorts of flavourings. It's a lot more stable than the egg-yolk variety, by which I mean that, once removed from the oven, it should stand for a good couple of minutes before starting to collapse.

Preheat the oven to 220°C/425°F/Gas Mark 7. Butter four 200 ml (7 fl oz) ramekins.

Pour the milk into a pan and bring to the boil. Meanwhile, whisk together the egg yolks and 35 g (1¼ oz) of the castor sugar until thick and creamy, then whisk in the flour. Pour the hot milk on to the egg mixture and whisk well, then return the custard to the pan and cook over a low heat until the mixture comes to the boil, stirring all the time. Remove from the heat, pour into a clean bowl and cover with cling film. Leave to cool to room temperature – the mixture must be cool but not cold.

Add the mashed banana to the cooled custard and whisk well.

Place the egg whites and cream of tartar in a very clean mixing bowl and whisk on a medium speed until the egg whites are thick and foamy (see page 129). Add the remaining 85 g (3 oz) of castor sugar and continue to whisk until glossy and fairly thick; do not over whisk or the finished soufflé will be hard and solid. Fold the meringue into the banana custard mixture.

Divide the mixture between the ramekins, place on a baking sheet and bake for 12–15 minutes, they will rise slowly at first but can then shoot up and overcook, so take care. Remove from the oven, dust with icing sugar and serve straight away.

baked vanilla
soufflé pudding

55 g (2 oz) unsalted butter

55 g (2 oz) plain white flour

300 ml (½ pint) whole milk

75 g (2¾ oz) castor sugar

15 ml (1 tablespoon) vanilla extract or powder

3 large eggs, separated

a pinch of cream of tartar

warm Caramelised Apricot Sauce (page 244), to serve

serves 6

It's not often you see a baked soufflé pudding like this any more, but they are a really nice change and very light. I cooked these at college years ago but I've updated the recipe, making the soufflé light and with the all-important 'wobble factor'.

All you need to do is turn the soufflé out and pour over warm caramelised apricot sauce.

Preheat the oven to 190°C/375°F/Gas Mark 5. Butter a 20 cm (8-inch) diameter, 11 cm (4½-inch) deep soufflé dish or Pyrex bowl.

Mix the butter and flour together to make a soft paste. Bring the milk to the boil, add the butter and flour mixture and whisk to bring back to the boil, then turn the heat down and stir over a low heat for 1 minute to cook the flour. Add 55 g (2 oz) of the castor sugar and the vanilla and stir well. Cover and leave for 20 minutes.

Whisk the egg whites with the cream of tartar on a medium speed until thick and foamy. Add the remaining 20 g (¾ oz) of castor sugar and continue to whisk until glossy and firm (see page 129).

Quickly stir the egg yolks into the milk mixture. Whisk half the meringue into the thick egg and milk mixture and then carefully fold in the remaining meringue. Spoon into the buttered dish.

Place the dish in a deep baking tray and fill the pan with enough cold water to come halfway up the side of the dish. Bake for 35–40 minutes or until well risen and golden brown on the top.

Remove from the oven, turn out carefully on to a large, warm serving plate and pour over the warm apricot sauce.

MERINGUES

There are many stories about the origin of meringues. The best one I have heard is that they were created in the early 1700s, quite by accident, by a baker who gently beat egg whites with a little sugar until they were thick and firm. He came from Meiringen in Switzerland – hence the name.

These 'drop scone' type meringues were often coloured very brightly with saffron or cochineal (crushed beetles) and they were greatly enjoyed throughout Europe and apparently by Marie Antoinette and the French court. It seems ironic that only a few hundred years earlier the French had declared sugar a poisonous and evil ingredient, and viewed it with great suspicion. Later on the piping bag was used to shape the meringue and all sorts of wonderful creations decorated banquets and state occasions.

The basic recipe is still the same – egg whites and sugar. The only addition I make is a little cream of tartar; this helps stabilise the basic structure of the meringue. If you don't have any cream of tartar, a little lemon juice is a good alternative. Add the cream of tartar or lemon juice to the egg whites at the very beginning, before you add the sugar. It ensures that the foam will not split or become grainy.

Sugars vary. I like to use a mixture of castor and icing for basic meringues; this gives the end product a smooth crumbly texture. Or I use Billington's unrefined sugars to give the meringue a slightly caramelly edge. You can just experiment with different sugars.

In this chapter you'll find (don't sneer) recipes for microwave meringues and directions for using packet meringue mixture (very handy if you are in trouble). Packet meringue mixture is available in most supermarkets, and I defy anybody to taste the difference once it's cooked or added to a mousse.

techniques

Whisking egg whites

It's important first of all to make sure that the bowl you are going to use and the whisk or beaters are spotlessly clean and dry, without a trace of grease, which can prevent the egg whites from whisking properly. Some people swear that a copper bowl can help the whites to increase in volume but china or glass ones are fine! The important thing is to pick a bowl that is big enough to whisk the requisite number of whites without bits of whisked mixture flying out everywhere.

Egg whites at room temperature whisk the best, I believe, and if they are a few days old, so much the better. But take care — if left uncovered for any length of time they can lose as much as 10 per cent moisture, making the end result softer and difficult to dry out. One chef friend of mine swears that frozen egg whites are the best for whisking.

Adding a pinch of cream of tartar to the whites helps to get the whites whisking up as well. Resist the temptation to add more cream of tartar. A pinch is all you need. It looks like nothing, but it will work, I promise. Too much cream of tartar will give the finished meringue a metallic aftertaste.

You can use a food mixer, a hand-held electric beater or a hand whisk, either rotary or a balloon whisk. If you're using a mixer or electric beater, then whisk on a medium speed – it takes slightly longer, but the whites won't separate so quickly.

Different stages of stiffness in whisking are suited to different recipes. Follow the recipe's instructions about the consistency you are aiming at. Generally, avoid over whisking egg whites, to the point at which they turn grainy. This is called 'break'.

Sugar

Measure the sugar carefully and add it at the correct point in the recipe. Many a recipe has been spoiled due to lack of attention to this.

Oven temperature

Oven temperature must be correct for each recipe. Too hot and the sugar will leach out and the meringues will darken. Too cold and the meringues will collapse and take forever to dry out.

see also

basic meringue

2 egg whites, at room temperature

a pinch of cream of tartar

55 g (2 oz) castor sugar

55 g (2 oz) icing sugar, sifted

Make sure the bowl and beaters you are using are spotlessly clean and grease-free, otherwise the egg whites may not whisk.

Place the egg whites and cream of tartar in a bowl or in a food mixer and whisk on a medium speed until they are thick and frothy but not grainy (see page 129). Add the castor sugar and whisk until very firm, thick and glossy.

Finally, remove the bowl from the machine and carefully fold in the sifted icing sugar.

packet meringue

275 g sachet of Supercook Whisk and
Bake Meringue Mix
25 g (1 oz) unrefined castor sugar
2.5 ml (½ teaspoon) vanilla powder

The reason I mention this very good product is it removes all problems with uncooked eggs because it's pasteurised, it's stable and works every time, and it's a very good substitute for Italian meringue. In Italian meringue, a boiling sugar syrup is whisked into egg whites, rather than just sugar and then the meringue is cooked so it sets firmly. This makes it safer for babies, the elderly and pregnant women to eat but, if you don't want to go to all the trouble of making your own, this product is a very good substitute in puddings and mousses.

Not many 'ready-made' products are of a really high quality, but this meringue, and good-quality pastry, are extremely good. Let the purists sneer, I bet they couldn't taste the difference when cooked.

Pour the sachet into a food mixer, add the sugar and whisk on a high speed for 15 minutes. Remove the bowl from the machine and fold in the vanilla powder.

That's it, simple, and stable.

gooseberry pavlova

500 g (1 lb 2 oz) ripe English gooseberries, topped and tailed

finely grated zest of 1 large lemon

55 g (2 oz) unrefined castor sugar

15–20 ml (3–4 teaspoons) cornflour, slaked in a little water

1 quantity basic meringue or a 275 g sachet of Supercook Whisk and Bake Meringue Mix

10 ml (2 teaspoons) cornflour

5 ml (1 teaspoon) white wine vinegar

5 ml (1 teaspoon) vanilla powder

600 ml (1 pint) double cream, very lightly whipped

serves 6–8

This is a simple and foolproof way of making pavlova. Much cooked and written about, this dessert now ranks alongside Poire Belle Hélène and Peach Melba in the famous pudding stakes.

A few years ago I went to New Zealand, the reputed home of pavlova, and probably ate this delightful pudding 30 times, and all, I might add perfect examples. The Kiwis like to fill their pavlovas rather predictably with either kiwifruit or passion-fruit, the acidity cutting not only the sweetness, but also the richness of the cream.

I do like to use English raspberries, but my all-time favourite just has to be gooseberries. The acidity and flavour of this wonderful, and under-used, British fruit is absolutely perfect. Gooseberries are only around for a short while so make the most of them. I have two bushes, and they always crop heavily, so I bag the fruit up and freeze it, so even at Christmas we can have gooseberry pavlova.

Heat the gooseberries in a pan with 15 ml (1 tablespoon) of cold water, the lemon zest and castor sugar. Cook until the fruit starts to soften and pop; this will take around 10 minutes.

Add the slaked cornflour, stirring all the time, to thicken. Remove from the heat and cool completely.

Preheat the oven to 140°C/275°F/Gas Mark 1. Lightly grease a baking sheet which is at least 30 cm (12 inches) square – the pavlova will spread when cooking. Mark out a 20 cm (8-inch) diameter circle on a piece of parchment or greaseproof paper (a plate is a good guide), turn upside-down and press on to the baking sheet. Re-grease very lightly.

Pour the meringue mix into the bowl of a food mixer and set the speed to medium. Whisk until glossy and firm – this will take about 10 minutes – then finish on the highest speed for a further 2 minutes. Add the cornflour, vinegar and vanilla powder and continue to whisk on high speed for 1 minute.

Spoon the meringue into the centre of the marked-out circle and, using a palette knife or the back of a large spoon, carefully spread the mixture to the edge of the circle. Try to keep the sides nice and high (remember, this will eventually hold a lot of gooseberry compote and cream) whilst creating an indentation in the centre – it sounds more difficult than it actually is, I promise. When you are happy, place the tray in the oven and cook for 1 hour. You will find the meringue will expand quite a lot, slightly colour and crack; this is normal.

After 1 hour, check the pavlova is cooked: it should be firm to the touch, yet crack if squeezed lightly, this ensures a soft marshmallowy inside, essential for a good pavlova (my mother just turns her oven off and leaves the pavlova to cool all night in the oven). Remove from the oven and cool.

To serve, carefully remove the meringue from the paper and place in the centre of a large serving plate.

Gently fold three-quarters of the gooseberry compote into the whipped cream, do not over mix as the acid from the gooseberries will thicken the cream and it's also nice to see a swirled effect. Spoon into the pavlova straight away, then drizzle over the remaining compote. Chill for 45 minutes – by this time the cream will have thickened slightly and you will be able to slice a nice wedge. That's it, just enjoy.

peppered clotted cream
meringues

150 g (5½ oz) granulated sugar

100 g (3½ oz) egg whites (about 3 egg whites), at room temperature

7.5 ml (1½ teaspoons) finely ground Sichuan pepper

5 ml (1 teaspoon) vanilla powder

clotted cream, to serve

unrefined icing sugar, to decorate

makes

about 16 meringues

These meringues use the Italian method of making meringue, that is, pouring boiling sugar over egg whites and whisking until very firm. The result is a very smooth meringue that does not collapse and is used a lot in the production of frozen and chilled mousses. Alternatively, you can use a ready-made variety (page 131).

The flavouring I am using here is Chinese Sichuan pepper, not normally used in sweet production. In fact, despite its name, this is not a pepper at all but the dried red berry from the ash tree. Its perfume is ideal not only for meringues but also with poached pears and peaches.

Preheat the oven to 120°C/250°F/Gas Mark ½. Cut two pieces of baking parchment to fit two large baking sheets. Fit a large piping bag with a 2 cm (¾-inch) piping nozzle.

Place the sugar and 100 ml (3½ fl oz) of cold water in a pan and bring to the boil. Place a sugar thermometer in the pan and then cook over a high heat until the syrup temperature reaches 120°C.

Start whisking the egg whites on high speed and gradually add the boiling sugar, pouring it down the inside of the bowl and trying to keep the sugar off the whisk itself. Once all the sugar syrup is in, whisk on a medium speed for about 12–14 minutes until very thick and glossy.

Stick the baking paper to the baking sheets with a small blob of meringue in each corner.

Carefully fold the Sichuan pepper and vanilla powder into the meringue. Fill the piping bag with the meringue and proceed to pipe about 32 small blobs of meringue the size of a 10p piece; try to keep them all the same size if possible.

Place in the oven and cook for about 2 hours to dry out – Italian meringue will dry a lot quicker than normal Swiss meringue. They should be a pale coffee colour. When cooked, remove from the oven and leave to cool.

To serve, sandwich two meringues together with a blob of clotted cream. Place in small paper cases and then dust with a little unrefined icing sugar.

baked alaska

3 large eggs, at room temperature

75 g (2¾ oz) castor sugar

75 g (2¾ oz) plain white flour, sifted

25 g (1 oz) unsalted butter, melted

for the filling

410 g can of peach slices in syrup, drained and syrup reserved

4 large egg whites, at room temperature

2 pinches of cream of tartar

115 g (4 oz) castor sugar

115 g (4 oz) icing sugar, sifted

lemon juice

500 g (1 lb 2 oz) vanilla ice cream, softened but not sloppy

10 glacé cherries

115 g (4 oz) angelica, cut into diamonds

½ orange, flesh scooped out carefully

castor sugar, to sprinkle

brandy, to serve

serves 6–8

One of my all-time favourites, the best ever, and it reminds me of my mum!

Preheat the oven to 200°C/400°F/Gas Mark 6. Lightly butter the inside of a 20 cm (8-inch) diameter × 7 cm (2¾-inch) deep cake tin, then chill.

Place the eggs and sugar in a bowl and whisk until thick and foamy, so the mixture holds its own weight (see page 276). Carefully fold in the sifted flour and then the melted butter. Pour into the chilled cake tin and place in the oven. Cook for 15 minutes or until the sponge is golden and risen and starts to shrink away from the side. Remove from the oven and cool.

Turn the sponge out of the tin and slice in half horizontally. Place the bottom half of the sponge on an ovenproof plate. Arrange the peaches on top and drizzle over a little syrup.

Increase the oven temperature to 230°C/450°F/Gas Mark 8. Whisk the egg whites with the cream of tartar in a food mixer using a medium speed, until thick and foamy (see page 129). Add the castor sugar and whisk again on a low speed until thick and glossy. Remove the bowl from the machine, fold in the icing sugar and a squeeze of lemon juice.

Spoon the ice cream on top of the peaches and top with the second piece of sponge. Spoon half of the meringue on to the sponge and very quickly spread all over the top and sides to seal. Smooth with a palette knife. Place the rest of meringue in a large piping bag fitted with a 1 cm (½-inch) fluted nozzle. Pipe a nice design over the cake and decorate with glacé cherries and angelica. Place the half-orange shell on top and carefully stick down with a blob of meringue. Sprinkle with a little castor sugar. Put the whole thing in the hot oven for 2–3 minutes to brown lightly and then remove from the oven.

Heat a little brandy in a ladle and pour into the half orange. Light and hey presto! Cut into large wedges and serve with double cream.

lime meringue pies

½ quantity shortbread pastry (page 45)
3 large eggs, separated, plus 1 additional
egg white

for the filling
115 g (4 oz) castor sugar
20 g (¾ oz) cornflour
40 g (1½ oz) unsalted butter
finely grated zest and juice of 3 large limes

for the meringue
a pinch of cream of tartar
115 g (4 oz) unrefined castor sugar
115 g (4 oz) unrefined icing sugar, sifted
granulated sugar, to decorate

makes

12 pies

Great finger food, the filling of these is made with cornflour so you can pick the pies up to eat easily.

Preheat the oven to 190°C/375°F/Gas Mark 5 and grease a 12-hole patty tin. Roll out the shortbread dough until it's about 2.5 mm (¼ inch) thick and then cut out twelve discs slightly larger than the patty tins themselves. Press a disc into each patty tin and then chill the tray well.

Cut small discs of greaseproof paper to line each patty tin individually. Press in lightly and then fill with baking beans. Place the tray on a baking sheet and bake for about 15–20 minutes, or until lightly browned. Keep an eye on them as they can burn very quickly indeed. Once cooked, remove from the oven and leave to cool until set. Do not try to remove the beans and paper until cool or you will end up tearing the fragile pastry.

For the filling, heat 125 ml (4 fl oz) of water and the castor sugar and bring to the boil. Remove from the heat. Slake the cornflour in 50 ml (2 fl oz) of water and add to the pan. Stir well, place the pan back on the heat and stir until it comes back to the boil, so the mixture thickens. The mixture will be very thick now, but don't worry. Add the butter and mix well until melted, then add the lime juice and zest, and finally the egg yolks. Stir well.

Leave the cooked pastry tarts in the baking tray. Spoon the lime filling into the cooked pastry tarts to fill them right up then leave to set thoroughly, which will take about 30 minutes at room temperature.

Turn up the oven to 220°C/425°F/Gas Mark 7. Whisk the egg whites with the cream of tartar using a medium speed, until thick and foamy (see page 129). Then add the castor sugar and continue to whisk until thick and glossy. Fold in the icing sugar.

Fit a large piping bag with a 1.5 cm (⅝-inch) piping nozzle, spoon in the meringue mixture and pipe it on to each tart with a nice design. Sprinkle over a little granulated sugar and bake for about 5–6 minutes, or until lightly browned and set. Allow to cool slightly before serving.

apricot daquaise

6 egg whites, at room temperature

a pinch of cream of tartar

150 g (5½ oz) castor sugar

150 g (5½ oz) sifted icing sugar

125 g (4½ oz) ground almonds

finely grated zest of 1 large lemon

600 ml (1 pint) double cream,
lightly whipped

8 fresh ripe apricots, halved and stoned,
halves cut into 4

icing sugar, to decorate

Caramelised Apricot Sauce,
to serve (page 244)

serves 4–6

This pudding must be chilled before serving so the meringue starts to break down and take on a gooey texture. A great summer dessert.

Preheat the oven to 140°C/275°F/Gas Mark 1. Fit a large piping bag with a 2 cm (¾-inch) plain nozzle. Lightly grease two baking sheets, then cut baking parchment to fit each sheet perfectly. Mark out three 18 cm (7-inch) diameter circles, two on one sheet and one on the other — a small plate is a perfect guide. Turn the paper over and press on to the trays.

Whisk the egg whites and cream of tartar together using a medium speed until thick and frothy (see page 129). Add the castor sugar and whisk on a high speed until you have a thick, glossy meringue. Carefully fold in the icing sugar and then the ground almonds.

Spoon the meringue into the piping bag and carefully pipe discs on the baking parchment, using the circles as a guide. The meringue can also be spooned out and then smoothed over with a palette knife if you don't fancy the piping.

Bake for 1½ hours, by which time the meringue should be set but still soft and a pale straw colour. When cooked, remove from the oven and leave to cool.

Carefully remove the meringues from the baking parchment and place one circle on the serving plate. Add the lemon zest to the whipped cream. Scatter half the apricots over one of the meringue circles, then top with half the cream. Place another meringue circle on top and repeat the process. Top with the last meringue disc and press down lightly. Chill for at least an hour.

Dust with icing sugar, cut into wedges and serve with a little apricot sauce.

POACHED
FRUIT &
COMPOTES

Poached, bottled and compote fruit became very close to my heart, after I watched the brilliant BBC series, *The Victorian Kitchen Garden* in the eighties. Since then I have been fascinated by how the Victorians grew and preserved fruits for the out-of-season months. They went to extraordinary lengths so they could always have fresh or preserved fruit on their dinner tables.

Many wealthy families had a town house and a country house, both of which needed supplying with fresh fruit, vegetables and flowers all year round. The head gardener and cook had to work very closely together not only in the planning and growing stages, but also to make sure everything was used. In times of heavy cropping the cook had to use the fruit immediately or preserve it, for the long or short term.

Fruits poached in a heavy syrup will keep for about a few days. If the fruit is to be kept any longer, then it needs to be bottled and sterilized. The Victorians pioneered this process and all manner of fruits were kept for the winter months.

These days, sadly, fruits seem to have no season. It's all too common to find supermarket shelves in winter groaning with strawberries, raspberries, plums and peaches. On one hand I agree that it's wonderful to have access to exotic ingredients from around the world and I understand that these fruits have to be grown wherever they happen to be in season and then transported, but all too often they're picked before they're ripe. The growers and supermarkets hope that they will ripen in transit or on the shelves. But the fruit's essential perfume, flavour, texture and, above all, sweetness develop in the very last stages of growth, when they're still on the tree, bush or vine.

I try not to play around too much with perfect, fresh, ripe fruit. There really is no point. I just enhance the flavour with a little sugar or a flavouring such as vanilla, elderflowers, fresh ginger, mint or alcohol. Nothing else is needed. The main thing is to serve all fresh fruit at room temperature.

In this chapter I explain how to poach, compote and bottle fruits. Some bottled fruits will keep for months, like the brandy kumquats or preserved clementines. The latter are an ideal alternative to Christmas pudding. English greengages (just as good as the French mirabelles in my opinion) are another fruit with a short season and therefore an ideal candidate for bottling. All currants bottle well especially with a dash of liqueur. I also touch on poaching quinces, cherries, figs, and even sweet pickled gooseberries for eating with vanilla ice cream. Soft fruits, such as strawberries and raspberries, are less successful when cooked: just enjoy them uncooked and in season.

techniques

Sterilising jars for preserves
If you are re-using jars, check for any chips or cracks and then wash the jars and remove any old labels. Rinse the jars well in hot water and turn upside-down to drain.

You can use a variety of methods to sterilise them.

Oven: put the jars on a rack or on a pad of kitchen paper on a tray and heat in the oven at 150°C/300°F/ Gas Mark 2 for 10 minutes or until thoroughly dry. Leave to cool.

Dishwasher: put the jars through a wash cycle to sterilise them ready for use.

Microwave: half fill the jars with water and heat on full power until the water boils. Use oven gloves to remove the jars from the oven, swirl the water round inside them, and then throw away the water and stand them upside-down on kitchen paper to drain thoroughly.

Saucepan: place the jars in a deep pan and cover with boiling water. Bring to the boil and boil for 10 minutes. Carefully remove and allow to drain and dry.

see also

muscat grapes warmed in vanilla butter and lemon oil *page 209*
warm pears with almonds and vanilla sugar *page 211*
sautéed apples in calvados *page 212*
sautéed bananas with brown sugar, lime and cream *page 213*
fresh pineapple with chilli and vanilla syrup *page 216*

poached peaches

with lime sabayon and shortbread

350 g (12 oz) castor sugar

zest of 1 lemon, removed with a peeler

4 ripe peaches

3 large egg yolks

50 ml (2 fl oz) dry white wine

55 g (2 oz) castor sugar

a squeeze of lime juice

45 ml (3 tablespoons) double cream

½ quantity My Mum's Shortbread
(page 298), to serve

serves 4

A simple but very nice pudding; it's best to start it the day before if you can, so the peaches have time to cool in the syrup. Not only does this help the removal of tough skins but it also adds flavour to the peaches, especially if they are slightly under-ripe. I always buy peaches by smell: if they smell good the chances are they will taste good.

I also tend to batch-cook peaches so I have plenty in stock, as they will keep perfectly in the syrup for a week in the fridge.

Place the sugar, 400 ml (14 fl oz) of cold water and lemon zest together in a pan and bring to the boil. Add the peaches and place a heatproof saucer on top to keep the peaches suspended under the syrup. Turn the heat down and gently simmer for 30 seconds, then turn the heat off and leave the peaches to cool in the syrup, preferably overnight. For this process to work the peaches have to be very ripe to begin with; if they are a little firm then just simmer for a couple of minutes instead of 30 seconds.

When cool, take the peaches out of the syrup and peel off their skins. Cut each peach in half and remove the stone, then drain on kitchen paper.

To make the sabayon, place the egg yolks, wine and sugar in a heatproof bowl and whisk over a pan of gently simmering water until thick, hot and foamy. Take off the pan and whisk on a high speed, with a hand-held whisk or in a food mixer, until thick, cold and creamy.

Add a squeeze of lime and the cream and stir – you should end up with a thick dropping consistency.

Sit the peach halves on plates, coat with sabayon and serve with the shortbread.

marinated peaches
with vanilla mascarpone

6 ripe peaches or nectarines

unrefined icing sugar, to taste

30–45 ml (2–3 tablespoons) peach liqueur

juice of 1 lime

60–75 ml (4–5 tablespoons) shredded fresh mint or lemon verbena

250 g (9 oz) mascarpone cheese

1 vanilla pod

serves 4

The secret here is to make sure the peaches are really ripe. I normally allow one and a half peaches per person.

Slice the peaches into wedges and lay on a ceramic or glass tray or bowl.

Sprinkle over unrefined icing sugar, drizzle over the liqueur and lime juice and finally sprinkle with the verbena or mint. Cover and leave to marinate for 2 hours minimum.

Beat the mascarpone with icing sugar to taste (it must not be too sweet).

Split the vanilla pod, scrape out the seeds carefully, add them to the mascarpone and mix well. You may want to add a touch of milk to make the end result a little lighter.

Spoon the peaches into dishes and serve with the vanilla mascarpone cream.

poached peaches
with lemon balm and bay syrup

4 ripe peaches or nectarines (they must be
ripe and smell beautifully sweet)
Lemon Balm and Bay Syrup (page 233)

serves 4

You'll find a picture of this recipe on page 232.

Place a small pan of water on the hob and bring to the boil and have ready a bowl of iced water. Once boiling, plunge the peaches, one at a time, into the water for 10–15 seconds – depending on the ripeness of the peach, the skin will come away very quickly indeed. Immediately remove from the water and place in the iced water to arrest the cooking. If the peaches are a little unripe then bring the water to the boil, add the peaches, top with a plate to keep the peaches suspended and leave to cool completely before you attempt to peel. Let the water come back to the boil, and repeat the process for the other three.

Carefully remove the skin from the peaches, discard the stones and slice into nice thick wedges. Arrange in a bowl.

Strain the syrup, pour over the peaches and chill for about 2 hours. Spoon over the syrup occasionally. Serve with clotted cream.

poached dried peaches
with mascarpone

2 lemons

350 g (12 oz) castor sugar

2 vanilla pods, split

250 g (9 oz) no-need-to-soak dried peaches

55 g (2 oz) unsalted butter

250 g (9 oz) mascarpone cheese, beaten,
to serve

serves 4

A quick but delicious dessert. The same recipe could be applied to any of the excellent semi-dried fruits now available.

Remove the zest from the lemons using a vegetable peeler and then squeeze the juice. Place the sugar and 600 ml (1 pint) of cold water in a saucepan, add the lemon zest and heat gently until the sugar has dissolved.

Add the juice to the syrup once it has dissolved and then simmer for 1 minute. Next add the vanilla pods and peaches and bring to the boil. Leave to cool and steep in the liquid, preferably overnight.

When you are ready to serve, gently warm through completely and then strain in a colander, reserving the syrup. Pour the syrup back into the saucepan and bring to the boil. Whisk in the butter until emulsified – the sauce should not be too thick and sugary so add a touch of water if necessary.

Divide the peaches between serving bowls and spoon over a little syrup. Serve warm, with a little beaten mascarpone.

poached dried apricots
in rosemary flower syrup

500 g (1 lb 2 oz) no-need-to-soak
dried apricots
finely grated zest and juice of 2 large limes
Rosemary Flower Syrup (page 231)

serves 4

This is very simple and a nice way to finish off a meal.

Place the apricots in a heatproof bowl. Strain the flowers out of the syrup, then bring the syrup to the boil in a small pan. Pour the syrup over the apricots, stir in the lime zest and juice and then tightly cover the bowl with cling film and leave to cool. Chill thoroughly, preferably overnight.

To serve, spoon the apricots into deep bowls and pour over a little of the syrup. Top with vanilla ice cream or beaten mascarpone.

amalfi lemon compote

1 large Amalfi lemon, or 3 large,
normal, unwaxed lemons
100 ml (3½ fl oz) water, plus extra
for blanching
heaped 30 ml (2 tablespoons) liquid glucose
115 g (4 oz) granulated sugar
2.5 ml (½ teaspoon) citric acid powder
5–10 ml (1–2 teaspoons) arrowroot, slaked
in a little water (optional)

We spent our honeymoon in Ravello, Italy, in the heart of the lemon-growing area. Everywhere we went we would come across huge amounts of Amalfi lemons and oranges. I was absolutely stunned at the size of the fruits when I first saw them they are enormous! I'm not kidding, the smallest are the size of a small grapefruit and the largest can be the size of a small football; they are quite unbelievable. So, I decided I needed to get to grips with cooking them pretty damn quickly.

The thought did cross my mind that they may be all skin and pith and have no substance whatsoever: how wrong I was, they were stunning. They are sweeter than any other lemon I have ever tasted (some people say that you can eat them like an orange, I think I may draw the line there). I have yet to find anybody who imports them but I'm on the look out, the sooner the better.

This compote is a real gem and I love it. It's great with raspberries, ice creams, meringues, pavlovas or even folded into crème fraîche.

Carefully peel the lemon(s) by hand using a sharp knife; remove all the pith, taking care not to pierce the flesh. Next, carefully remove as much of the white pith from the skin as possible and discard, then chop the zest into 5 mm (¼-inch) pieces. Chop the flesh, retaining as much of the juice as possible.

Put the zest into a pan, cover with cold water and bring to the boil. Once boiling, strain well through a sieve. Return the zest to the pan, cover with fresh cold water again and repeat the process.

Now put the blanched zest and lemon flesh into a clean pan, add 100 ml (3½ fl oz) of cold water, and the glucose, sugar and citric acid and bring to the boil. Gently simmer for about 20–30 minutes, or until the liquor has reduced and thickened slightly. I tend to thicken the mixture a touch with a little arrowroot or cornflour at this point – the secret is not to thicken it too much. Normally I would expect to use about a teaspoon of arrowroot or cornflour for the above amount.

Pour into a small, sterilised (page 149) preserving jar and refrigerate for at least 2 weeks to mature.

new-season rhubarb
poached in dry vermouth and cinnamon

350 g (12 oz) new-season rhubarb

450 ml (16 fl oz) Noilly Prat or other dry white vermouth

350 g (12 oz) castor sugar

1 vanilla pod, split

1 cinnamon stick

10 ml (2 teaspoons) finely chopped fresh root ginger

serves 4

I really look forward to the 'forced' new-season rhubarb, it's about the only decent colour you can get in Britain in February and March (apart from Seville oranges). The forced variety is quite delicate and seems to need gentle handling and flavours, so light poaching in syrup marries perfectly.

I also like the thick-stemmed reddy-green home-grown variety which has a slightly tarter flavour and is much nicer in pies, puddings, ice creams and sorbets.

Wash, then top and tail the rhubarb and cut into 2.5 cm (1-inch) pieces.

Pour the vermouth into a saucepan add the sugar, vanilla pod and cinnamon stick and bring to the boil. Gently simmer for 1 minute until the sugar has dissolved, then add the rhubarb and ginger and stir well. Simmer for 1 minute then remove from the heat.

Tip into a large bowl, cover with cling film and leave to cool. Serve with Champagne Sabayon (page 236) or vanilla ice cream.

new-season rhubarb soup
with honeycomb

450 g (1 lb) forced rhubarb, cut into 3 cm
(1½-inch) pieces

finely grated zest and juice of 1 lime

115 g (4 oz) golden, unrefined castor sugar

200 ml (7 fl oz) dry vermouth

1 comb of honey (Tiptree sell a 340 g jar,
with the comb set in acacia honey)

200 g (7 oz) crème fraîche

serves 4

Yorkshire produces a third of the world's rhubarb and, at the time of writing we are just about to start the season. Forced rhubarb is grown in huge sheds in almost total darkness; this process produces pale pink, subtly flavoured, tender stems. This rhubarb is excellent for poaching with a little white wine or vermouth, for making a delicate sorbet or beautifully coloured jelly or it can be mixed with custard to make a gorgeous fool.

Maincrop rhubarb, grown outside and later on in the year, lends itself better to pies, crumbles, jams and pickles.

Rhubarb marries very well with rich foods such as wild duck and, served in ketchup form, with scallops.

Place the rhubarb, lime zest and juice and castor sugar in a stainless steel pan. Put the lid on and cook for about 5 minutes, so the juices start to run and the rhubarb begins to break down. Add the vermouth, bring to the boil and continue to cook for a further 10 minutes or until the rhubarb is cooked.

Liquidise the rhubarb and juice together until very smooth, then pass through a fine sieve. Keep warm.

Meanwhile carefully cut the comb honey into small chunks, add to the crème fraîche and just gently stir together so you can still see the comb.

To serve, swirl some crème fraîche into the warm rhubarb soup. If you have a sweet tooth, then you may want to add a little more sugar.

blackcurrant liqueur compote

350 g (12 oz) firm English blackcurrants

200 g (7 oz) golden castor sugar

100 ml (3½ fl oz) good-quality Cassis

makes

about 500 ml (16 fl oz)

Great with lemon ice cream, hot sponge puddings or even egg custard tart.

Pick over the blackcurrants and remove any stalks or damaged currants and then wash and drain well. Place in a pan with the sugar and 200 ml (7 fl oz) of cold water and bring to a gentle boil. Simmer gently until the fruit is soft and thick but not too broken up. Remove from the heat, stir in the liqueur and place in a clean, hot, sterilised preserving jar (see page 149). Seal.

Using a pan which is deep enough to allow the jar to be covered completely with cold water, put a folded tea towel in the bottom of the pan so the glass is not in direct contact with the metal and then put the jar in the pan and cover with cold water. Lay a sugar or cooking thermometer on top of the jar.

Gently heat the water so it takes 1½ hours to reach 90°C. Once up to temperature, turn the heat down and hold the temperature at 90°C for 15 minutes exactly.

Carefully lift the jars out using gloves or tongs (take care not to drop them as they are very slippery and hot) and place on a wooden chopping board or cloth, never on a metal or cold surface as the sudden change in temperature will make the glass crack. Leave to cool and then store in a cool, dark place. If sterilised correctly, the compote will keep for months.

poached damsons

400 g (14 oz) ripe English damsons

250 g (9 oz) unrefined granulated sugar

a pinch of citric acid powder (optional)

juice and finely grated zest of 2 large lemons

serves 4

My love of damsons began when I worked in the Lake District in the early eighties. All our damsons came from an area just outside Kendal called the Lythe valley.

We would buy huge amounts to convert into jam or jelly, for bottling and even for relishes to serve with ham baked in stout. I once recall reading a very old Lake District recipe for damson sauce with baked char, a beautiful fish only found in Windermere: damson is a wonderfully versatile fruit.

This area has been growing damsons since about 1870 and in those days nearly all the picked fruit was transported to Yorkshire. Over the years, many of the original damson trees have disappeared but, thankfully, you can still buy damsons from the Lythe valley.

Lightly poached in a sugar syrup, damsons are delicious, with the added bonus that you don't have to stone them.

Wash the damsons well in plenty of cold water and remove any stalks.

Place the sugar and citric acid with 450 ml (16 fl oz) of cold water in a pan and bring to the boil to dissolve the sugar. Once dissolved, add the damsons, bring back to the boil then gently simmer for 30 seconds. Transfer to a bowl, cover with cling film and leave to cool. Chill well.

Once chilled, stir in the lemon juice and zest. Serve with vanilla or Rich Lemon Curd Ice Cream (page 175) or thick double cream.

poached custard apples
with vanilla, brown sugar and beaumes de venise

2 large, ripe custard apples

55 g (2 oz) unsalted butter

30–40 ml (6–8 teaspoons) soft brown sugar

1 vanilla pod, split

100 ml (3½ fl oz) Beaumes de Venise or another good-quality dessert wine

serves 4

Though not often used by chefs, custard apples are very nice to cook with. Cherimoya – another name for custard apples – is a fruit that really is delicious on its own, provided it's ripe; it needs very careful handling as it bruises easily.

The taste is like nothing else, buttery with a hint of vanilla, but the seeds are inedible, so try to remove as many as possible when you've sliced the fruit.

The less you play around with a fruit like this the better. Here I just warm it in a little butter, wine and sugar. Take care not to overcook.

Cut each apple into 6–8 wedges and carefully remove the pips whilst trying to keep the fruit as whole as possible.

Heat the butter in a wok until it just begins to brown and foam, then add the sugar and vanilla pod and stir in. Pop in the apple slices and gently warm through on both sides, then add the wine and bring to the boil.

Take off the heat and allow to stand for 2–3 minutes. Spoon into bowls and pour over the glorious buttery juices. You can scoop a large ball of vanilla ice cream on top if you wish.

poached cherries

500 g (1 lb 2 oz) ripe, deep red
English cherries
250 g (9 oz) granulated sugar
a pinch of citric acid powder (available
from pharmacies, optional)
juice and finely grated zest of 2 large lemons

serves 4

There is no real mystery to poaching fruits, the only thing to watch is the cooking time: a few seconds, coupled with cooling down in the syrup, is plenty to soften beautifully ripe fruit.

English cherries are only available for a few weeks, so enjoy them.

The tedious part of this recipe is the stoning of the cherries, but it has to be done. Once that is out of the way, place the sugar, 400 ml (14 fl oz) of cold water and citric acid in a pan and bring to the boil. Once the sugar has dissolved, add the cherries and bring back to the boil, then simmer gently for 30 seconds. Pour into a bowl, cover with cling film and leave to cool; then chill well.

When chilled, remove the cling film and stir in the lemon juice and zest. Spoon into bowls, top with clotted cream and serve with shortbread (page 298).

bottled greengages
with lemon

18 ripe, unblemished and firm greengages

250 g (9 oz) granulated sugar

4 thick slices of lemon

makes

about 750 ml (1¼ pints)

As apprentices, we would cook and bottle hundreds of greengages but, sadly, chefs these days don't use this delicious British fruit much.

I say British fruit but it was actually brought back from France in the late eighteenth century by a certain Sir William Gage, and has been a favourite ever since. I love greengage jam, which is an essential part of Fern's Queen of Puddings (page 22). The same method can be applied to plums and apricots.

Sterilise the preserving jars and rubber rings (see page 149) and have the jars wet so the gages slide down inside them easily.

Pick over the fruit and remove any stalks. Cut the fruit in half and remove the stones.

Bring the sugar and 250 ml (9 fl oz) of cold water to the boil together and then leave to cool.

Carefully pack the fruit into the jar, pour over the syrup to cover and finally add the lemon slices. Seal the jars.

You now need to use a pan which is deep enough to allow the bottles to be covered completely with cold water – put a folded tea towel in the bottom of the pan so the glass is not in direct contact with the metal and then put the jars in the pan and cover with cold water. Lay a sugar or cooking thermometer on top of the jars.

Gently heat the water so it takes 1½ hours to reach 90°C. Once the temperature is 90°C, turn the heat down and hold at this temperature for 15 minutes exactly.

Carefully lift the jars out using gloves or tongs and place on a wooden chopping board or cloth, never on a metal or cold surface or the sudden change in temperature will make the glass crack. Leave to cool and then store in a cool, dark place; they will keep indefinitely.

To serve, spoon greengages into deep bowls and top with clotted cream.

preserved clementines
in brandy

8 large sweet, juicy clementines

225 g (8 oz) castor sugar,

2 vanilla pods, split

juice and finely grated zest of 2 lemons

150 ml (¼ pint) brandy

These are a great Christmas treat. When you are fed up with lashings of turkey, pudding, trifles, nuts, the obligatory Quality Street and all the rest of it, these whole preserved clementines are just the ticket: they are quite tart and juicy and partner a large blob of home-made vanilla ice cream extremely well. They also keep well in a sealed jar in a fridge for weeks.

Preheat the oven to 160°C/325°F/Gas Mark 3. Pick over the clementines and make sure there are no blemishes or rotting skins. Place them in a pan and cover with cold water. Bring to the boil, then strain into a colander. Put the clementines back into the pan, refill with cold water then bring to the boil again. Repeat this process twice more and then, on the final time, gently simmer for about 10 minutes, then strain.

Carefully cut the clementines in half (they will be very hot indeed) and place, cut-side down, in a shallow, non-metallic baking dish.

Bring 250 ml (9 fl oz) of water to the boil with the castor sugar until the sugar has dissolved. Add the vanilla pods and gently simmer for about 2–3 minutes. Pour over the clementines and loosely cover with foil, then place the dish in the oven and cook for about 35–40 minutes.

Carefully remove the dish from the oven and take the foil off, return to the oven and turn up the heat to about 200°C/400°F/Gas Mark 6. Cook until the syrup has reduced by about half to a quarter and is nice and thick. Remove from the oven, spoon some of the syrup over each of the clementines and leave to cool completely.

When cool, pack into a sterilised jar (see page 149) along with the vanilla pods. Stir the lemon juice and zest and brandy into the syrup and pour over the fruit. Seal the jar and store in the fridge. Serve with vanilla ice cream.

bottled kumquats
with armagnac

600 g (1 lb 5 oz) kumquats

350 g (12 oz) light brown soft sugar

juice of 1 lemon

45 ml (3 tablespoons) Armagnac

makes

two 500 ml (18 fl oz) jars

Most of the time I really don't know what to do with kumquats because they can be rather unpleasant actually – bitter, sour and hard. For me, the only way to cook them is to soften them in a jar with sugar and Armagnac, then at last they are edible, and very nice they are too!

They make a great Christmas present and are also very nice to eat in January and February when you're fed up with the cold, wet, rainy days. I eat mine with a large cappuccino after a heavy meal.

Sterilise two 500 ml (18 fl oz) preserving jars and their sealing rings (see page 149). Wash the fruits well and remove any stalks.

Boil the sugar and 400 ml (14 fl oz) of cold water together until the sugar has dissolved and then leave to cool.

Stir in the lemon juice and Armagnac. Wet the preserving jars, divide the fruit between them, then pour in the syrup. Seal the jars.

You now need to use a pan which is deep enough to allow the jars to be covered completely with cold water – put a folded tea towel in the bottom of the pan so the glass is not in direct contact with the metal then put the jars in the pan and cover with cold water. Lay a sugar or cooking thermometer on top of the jars.

Gently heat the water so it takes 1½ hours to reach 90°C. Once the temperature is 90°C, turn the heat down and hold the temperature at 90°C for 15 minutes exactly.

Carefully lift the jars out using gloves or tongs and place on a wooden chopping board or cloth, never on a metal or cold surface or the sudden change in temperature will make the glass crack. Leave to cool and then store in a cool, dark place. If bottled correctly, these will keep in a cool place indefinitely.

poached pears

with spices and chilli

1 small red chilli

5 ml (1 teaspoon) whole cloves

5 ml (1 teaspoon) garam masala

½ cinnamon stick

350 g (12 oz) castor sugar

1 lime

6 ripe pears

serves 6

A nice way to end a heavy meal. Remember that the chilli is a seasoning, so a little will go a long way.

Cut the chilli in half lengthways and discard the seeds, then place in a large pan with the cloves, garam masala and cinnamon stick. Add the sugar and 600 ml (1 pint) of cold water, bring to the boil and simmer until the sugar dissolves. Cut the lime in half, squeeze the juice into the pan and then add the lime halves. Simmer for 30 seconds and then remove from the heat.

Carefully peel the pears using a potato peeler. Using a small, sharp knife, work up from the base to make a narrow tunnel and remove the core, but leave the pears whole.

Add the pears to the hot syrup and bring back to the boil, then remove the pan from the heat. Cover and leave the pears to cool in the syrup.

To finish, serve the whole cool pears in a bowl and spoon over some of the syrup. Serve with thick cream.

ICE CREAM & PARFAITS

Ice cream has been around for centuries, and was supposedly invented by the Italians. I'm not too sure about this, but they were certainly amongst the first to sell ice cream on street corners. In those days it was a sort of crunchy honeycomb ice cream now very popular in New Zealand where it's called Hokey Pokey.

English cooks also made ice cream. Some of our great country houses had ice caves to store ice in the winter, so come spring and summer ice creams could still be made. The Victorians adored ice cream and sherbets and consumed huge amounts. It was the thing at the time to have a continental chef and these chefs brought new and exciting ice creams to the tables of the very rich. My old college lecturer, Brian, told me fascinating stories of how they used to cut ice from the lochs near Balmoral to store covered with ferns in caves to make the Queen's ice cream in the summer months. Of course it was all churned by hand; it must have been really hard work.

In Britain we are one of the biggest producers of ice cream in the world, with thousands of flavours. We Brits eat an average of 15 kg each of the stuff every year; only the Americans eat more.

I still have fond memories of Mr Whippy and his weird musical van. Though it's not what the purists call ice cream, there was something strangely comforting and delicious about the stuff, especially when it was covered in 'monkey's blood' (raspberry sauce to you and me). Even now I really, really like the creamy, soft texture with a couple of flakes; so do the kids.

Parfaits are close cousins of ice cream. There are two sorts: the boiled sugar version and the meringue variety. Parfaits lend themselves to an enormous range of interesting flavours and I've included some real winners here, from

malt loaf to caramelised croissant. The other great thing about parfaits is that you don't need an ice-cream machine to make them. For the recipes that need to be made in a machine, all are suitable for a 1.2-litre (2-pint) ice-cream maker.

techniques

Making caramel

Place the sugar in a heavy-based, preferably non-stick pan and add just enough cold water to cover, or follow the recipe instructions for adding water or not.

Using a pastry brush and a little more cold water, brush down into the sugar water any sugar crystals sticking to the pan side; this is very important as, if you do not do this, grains of sugar can fall back into the boiling sugar and cause the whole thing to crystallise. This might not matter for caramel but if you are attempting any kind of spun-sugar decoration or making sweets like humbugs, it's vital you avoid this, so get into the habit of brushing down the sides until the water and sugar have been boiling for at least 5 minutes.

Now place the pan over a fairly high heat and bring to the boil quickly. Keep washing down the edges and keep it at boiling point; the syrup will thicken gradually and start to turn a very pale amber. Keep watching it all the time.

Follow the recipe instructions for how dark a caramel you are aiming at. The rule is, the lighter the colour, the sweeter the taste will be.

If the recipe requires more water to be added to the finished caramel to dissolve it to make caramel syrup, put the water in a jug and tip it carefully into the hot caramel. There will be a lot of spluttering and splashing so stand back from it and don't worry. Bring the caramel syrup back to the boil to allow any pieces of caramel to melt, stirring occasionally. Then pour into a jug and allow to cool a little or use as the recipe directs.

custard base
for ice cream

250 ml (9 fl oz) whole milk

1 vanilla pod, split

4 egg yolks

55 g (2 oz) castor sugar

makes

about 225 ml (8 fl oz)

Good ice creams need a good base and this is it; it's relatively simple. Make it and pop it in the fridge for up to four days and then just knock up the ice cream when you are ready.

Place the milk and vanilla pod in a pan and bring to the boil.

Whisk the egg yolks and sugar together until fairly pale; there is no need to go mad!

When the milk is simmering, pour it carefully over the whisked egg and sugar. Whisk well and return to the pan.

Cook over a low heat, stirring constantly, until thickened. This may take a few seconds or a couple of minutes so just keep an eye on the custard to make sure it does not get too hot and curdle.

Remove from the heat and strain through a fine sieve to remove the vanilla pod and any pieces of over-cooked egg. Cover and allow to cool. Ready to go!

vanilla ice cream

225 ml (8 fl oz) custard base for ice cream
(opposite)
250 ml (9 fl oz) double cream
250 ml (9 fl oz) stock syrup (page 190)
serves 4–6

This is a very smooth, sweet, velvety-rich, classic ice cream, perfect not only with warm summer strawberries or raspberries, or with sliced plums or peaches, but also with apple pie, or steamed hazelnut or sticky toffee puddings.

If you are going to eat this ice cream with any fruit, don't automatically sweeten the fruit but taste first: the ice cream will probably be sweet enough.

If you like your ice cream a little less sweet, add only about 150 ml (¼ pint) of stock syrup instead of the whole amount. This means the finished product will lose some of its velvety texture, though, so be careful not to reduce it too much.

Place a container in the freezer to pre-chill. Once the custard base is cool, add the double cream and stock syrup and whisk well. Pour into an ice-cream machine and churn following the ice-cream-maker's instructions until thick and creamy – this ice cream will not set too firmly, so remove it from the machine when very thick and velvety. Transfer to the chilled container and store in the freezer for up to two weeks.

chocolate ripple ice cream
To make chocolate ripple ice cream, carefully pour 115 g (4 oz) of melted bitter chocolate in a thin, steady stream into the ice cream once it has been churned in the machine – the chocolate will set upon contact with the ice cream and break up. Churn for a further 10 seconds and then transfer to a container and store in the freezer for up to two weeks.

caramel ice cream

125 g (4½ oz) castor sugar

225 ml (8 fl oz) custard base for ice cream
(page 172)

275 ml (9½ fl oz) double cream

225 ml (8 fl oz) stock syrup (page 190)

1.25 ml (¼ teaspoon) salt

serves 4–6

The thing to remember with anything to do with caramel is to make sure the sweetness is not too intense. Caramel by its very nature is sweet, but it's amazing how, as the sugar darkens, the caramel becomes less sweet. Years ago, almost black caramel known as 'black jack' was actually used to darken gravies and sauces – caramel can be extremely bitter.

For this recipe, make sure the caramel is very dark (not black) and, coupled with a little salt – yes, salt! – this ice cream will have a nice sharp caramel flavour, and finish up as smooth as silk.

The recipe does need an ice-cream machine to get a perfect result but you will not taste a better caramel ice cream anywhere.

Place a container in the freezer to pre-chill. The first thing is to make the caramel (see page 171). Place the sugar in a thick-bottomed pan and barely cover with cold water. Bring to the boil and cook rapidly until very dark, but not black. At this point add 75 ml (2½ fl oz) of cold water and stand back, the caramel will boil and splutter furiously, take care and don't panic, just let it bubble for a minute and then swirl the pan around to dissolve the caramel. Pour into a bowl or jug to cool; you will end up with a thick caramel syrup.

Place the cooled custard, cream, stock syrup, salt and caramel in a bowl and stir well together. Pour this mixture into an ice-cream machine and churn until thick and smooth.

Transfer to the pre-chilled container and store in the freezer for a couple of weeks.

rich lemon curd
ice cream

225 ml (8 fl oz) custard base for ice cream
(page 172)

300 ml (½ pint) double cream

310 g jar of good-quality lemon curd

finely grated zest and juice of 1 large lemon

candied orange zest, to decorate

serves 4–6

The wonderful thing about this ice cream is that you can really adapt it for any curd you want with a delicious result. This is a very simple and quick recipe, I promise.

I buy my lemon curd, purely because it's easier but, if you want to go the whole hog and make your own that is up to you. If not, make sure you buy a good quality curd.

Passion-fruit, banana and orange curds all make great ice cream. Just remember that, if you are going to make a curd ice cream, you will need to add extra juice and zest of your chosen fruit to your ice cream. This will ensure a deep-tasting, powerful ice cream

I like to serve this ice cream with Caramel Mousse (page 104) and candied orange zest. To make the candied orange zest, remove the zest from two large oranges using a sharp knife, taking great care not to include any pith. Slice finely and then cover with cold water in a small pan. Bring to the boil, strain well and repeat twice more. To the zest, add 115 ml (4 fl oz) of cold water, 115 g (4 oz) of granulated sugar and 15 ml (1 tablespoon) of liquid glucose. Bring to the boil and then simmer very gently for about 25 minutes. The zest should be soft and succulent. Drain well and leave to dry, spread out on baking parchment, in a warm place. Store in an airtight jar, sprinkled with a little castor sugar.

Place a container in the freezer to pre-chill. Pour the custard, cream and lemon curd into a clean bowl and whisk together. Add the lemon zest and juice and mix well.

Place in the ice-cream maker and churn according the instructions until very thick. Remove from the machine and spoon into the pre-chilled container. Freeze for 30 minutes and then eat or keep in the freezer for a up to a couple of weeks

caramel pecan
ice cream

115 g (4 oz) pecans

85 g (3 oz) granulated sugar

250 ml (9 fl oz) whole milk

1 vanilla pod, split

4 egg yolks

3 pinches of salt

55 g (2 oz) castor sugar

1 gelatine leaf, soaked in cold water

250 ml (9 fl oz) double cream

150 ml (¼ pint) stock syrup (page 190)

serves 4–6

One of the nicest ice creams, not just because I love to eat great bowlfuls, but also because it is good accompanying other desserts, such as cheesecakes, fruit compotes, pancakes, sponges, cakes and meringues with clotted cream.

The two things to remember are to roast the pecans first in a moderate oven to release their unique flavour, and the addition of salt. This balances the whole ice cream, cutting the sweetness amazingly. You would never notice the saltiness if I had not told you about it but it is vital to the balanced, finished product.

You will see that I have added gelatine: if this ice cream is kept in the freezer for more than a day or two, gelatine helps to set the weeping sugar whilst the ice cream is frozen and also helps stop the ice cream collapsing in a warm environment when serving.

Preheat the oven to 220°C/425°F/Gas Mark 7. Place a container in the freezer to pre-chill. Place the pecans on a metal baking tray and roast for 10 minutes until nicely browned all over. Remove and cool. Do use the oven: toasting under a grill tends to brown the nuts unevenly and burns them very quickly.

Place the granulated sugar in a shallow pan and cook over a moderate heat until light brown (see page 171). Add the pecans and stir. Cook for 2–3 minutes and then tip out on to well oiled greaseproof paper and leave to cool completely. Chop into chunks the size of a thumbnail (don't do this in the processor as this just turns the caramel pecans into powder)

Place the milk and vanilla pod in a saucepan and bring to the boil gently.

Meanwhile, whisk together the egg yolks, salt and castor sugar until just pale (do not overdo it). Pour on the boiling milk, whisk and return to the pan. Cook over a low heat, stirring continuously, until thickened, and then add the soaked gelatine. Strain the mixture and cool.

Once cool, add the double cream and stock syrup, mix well and place in the ice-cream machine. Churn to the maker's instructions until the ice cream is soft and silky, then add the chopped pecan and caramel crunch and mix well. Spoon into the chilled container, cover and store in the freezer. This

ice cream keeps for about 3–4 days but, after this time, the caramel will begin to weep, which spoils the appearance though it doesn't affect the taste.

christmas pudding
ice cream

185 ml (6½ fl oz) stock syrup (page 190)

1 cinnamon stick

2.5 ml (½ teaspoon) ground mixed spice

85 g (3 oz) Christmas pudding, chopped into small pieces

30 ml (2 tablespoons) brandy

225 ml (8 fl oz) custard base for ice cream (page 172)

150 ml (¼ pint) double cream

serves 4–6

If you are not too keen on Christmas pudding on its own, this may be for you. Not too rich, easy to make and can be made well in advance – plus, the kids will eat it.

If you really do not like Christmas pudding, a good fruit cake soaked in a little brandy is a good alternative.

Place a container in the freezer to pre-chill.

Warm the stock syrup in a small pan, add the cinnamon stick and mixed spice, remove from the heat and leave to cool and infuse for 15 minutes.

Meanwhile, soak the Christmas pudding in the brandy.

Mix the custard with the cream. Strain the stock syrup to remove the cinnamon and add to the cream mixture. Mix in the Christmas pudding and brandy.

Churn in an ice-cream-maker until thick and frozen and then transfer to the chilled container and store in the freezer for up to a couple of weeks. Serve with a large glass of brandy and Brandy Snaps (page 291).

nutmeg ice cream

225 ml (8 fl oz) custard base for ice cream
(page 172)
250 ml (9 fl oz) stock syrup (page 190)
250 ml (9 fl oz) double cream
heaped 10 ml (2 teaspoons) grated nutmeg
(about 1 whole nutmeg)

serves 6–8

I started to make this ice cream way back in 1990; a lot of people have since made their own versions but to me this is the only way to do it. A slightly unusual ice cream but it works very well with baked egg custard tart, a combination that won me 'Dessert Chef of the Year'.

I like to eat this ice cream in autumn and winter, with apples, pears, quinces and plums. I think it's a little too strong for summer fruits.

The last thing I would say is always grate fresh nutmegs for this, as the delicate perfume of nutmeg deteriorates very quickly.

Place a container in the freezer to pre-chill. Place all the ingredients in a bowl and mix well. Pour into an ice-cream maker and churn until thick.

Remove, transfer to the pre-chilled container and store in the freezer for up to two weeks.

punch parfait

200 ml (7 fl oz) dry red wine

200 ml (7 fl oz) strong cold tea

200 ml (7 fl oz) freshly squeezed
orange juice

juice of 2 lemons

200 ml (7 fl oz) castor sugar

1 cinnamon stick

6 cloves

6 allspice berries

2 large eggs, plus 2 large egg yolks

60 ml (4 tablespoons) dark rum

55 g (2 oz) castor sugar

250 ml (9 fl oz) double cream,
lightly whipped

serves 6–8

I got the idea for this dessert years ago when working for a German chef who used to love Glühwein when he was out skiing; when he came back to England, he used to make it in the kitchen on cold days. The smell of the warm red wine, cloves, cinnamon and citrus fruits is one of the most welcoming I know. Needless to say, we always had plenty left over, so, as I hate waste, I devised this parfait recipe.

The added bonus is that you do not need an ice-cream machine, just a freezer and a plastic tub!

Firstly put a 2-litre (3½-pint) plastic container and lid in a freezer to chill well.

Pour the red wine, tea, orange juice, lemon juice, castor sugar, cinnamon stick, cloves, and allspice into a measuring jug, and make a note of the total amount. Pour this mixture into a pan and bring to the boil, stirring to dissolve the sugar. Once boiling, turn down the heat and continue to simmer rapidly to reduce the liquid until you have only one-quarter of the original volume (make sure you measure it exactly). Do take care not to burn the liquid as it has quite a lot of sugar in it. Strain the reduced liquid and allow to cool.

Put the eggs, egg yolks, rum and castor sugar in a heatproof bowl and whisk over a pan of gently simmering water until thick and foamy. Transfer the egg mixture to a food-mixer bowl and whisk at high speed until cold and thick.

The rest is easy! Gently fold the cooled sugar reduction into the egg mixture with a whisk and then carefully fold in the whipped cream. Remove the ice-cold container from the freezer, fill with the parfait and freeze until set, overnight if possible. It can be kept frozen for up to two weeks. Serve with fingers of My Mum's Shortbread (page 298).

poppy seed and cinnamon
parfait

35 g (1¼ oz) poppy seeds

100 ml (3½ fl oz) whole milk

1 cinnamon stick

4 large egg yolks, plus 1 large egg

2 pinches of ground cinnamon

150 g (5½ oz) castor sugar

30 ml (2 tablespoons) dark rum

300 ml (½ pint) double cream,
lightly whipped

serves 6–8

This unusual parfait is very simple to make and perfect with poached fruits such as cherries, plums, peaches and even Medjool dates. Its dense texture and distinct flavour are a real joy to eat and one of my favourites from years ago.

Wet a 450 g (1 lb) loaf tin and line it with cling film. Lightly grind the poppy seeds with a rolling pin on a chopping board or in a pestle and mortar. Alternatively, you could grind them in a spice grinder; take care, though, as all you want is to crush them enough to get the flavour out, not to reduce them to powder.

Place them in a saucepan and add the milk and cinnamon stick. Bring to the boil and cover and leave to simmer for 10 minutes. Strain through a fine sieve, reserving the seeds.

Place the egg yolks, egg, ground cinnamon, sugar and rum in a heatproof bowl and, using an electric hand-whisk, whisk over a pan of gently simmering water until thick, cooked and foamy (this will take about 10 minutes).

Pour the mixture into the bowl of a food mixer if possible, and whisk on a high speed until cold and very thick. Fold the egg mixture into the whipped cream, along with the poppy seeds.

Spoon into the lined loaf tin, cover with another piece of cling film and freeze overnight or keep in the freezer for up to a couple of weeks.

The next day, turn the parfait out of the tin, remove the cling film and cut into thick slices.

rhubarb parfait

400 g (14 oz) new-season rhubarb, cut into
2 cm (¾-inch) pieces
juice of 1 large lemon
4 egg whites, at room temperature
2 pinches of cream of tartar
200 g (7 oz) unrefined castor sugar
300 ml (½ pint) double cream,
lightly whipped

makes

two 450 g (1 lb) loaf tins

It's quite difficult to halve this recipe so I make two parfaits – and I can guarantee you that they won't stay in the freezer very long once you have tasted this very subtle and very easy parfait.

Forced (new-season) rhubarb is the best for this parfait, maincrop tends to be very green and doesn't have the subtlety of flavour, or the impact of colour, that new-season rhubarb possesses.

Lightly wet two 450 g (1 lb) loaf tins and then line with cling film. Place the rhubarb and lemon juice in a pan and cook over a low heat for 10 minutes until you have a stringy purée. Remove from the heat and allow to cool.

Whisk the egg whites with the cream of tartar on a medium speed until thick and foamy (see page 129). Add the castor sugar and continue to whisk on a medium speed until firm and glossy, but do not over whisk.

Fold the cooled purée into the egg whites and then quickly fold this mixture into the double cream before the acid from the rhubarb curdles the cream. Spoon into the lined loaf tins, smooth out the top to flatten, then cover with cling film and freeze overnight or keep for up to two weeks.

To serve, unwrap and cut into thick slices. Serve with a little poached rhubarb and Macaroons (page 133).

malt loaf parfait

175 g (6 oz) malt loaf

8 eggs, separated

250 g (9 oz) unrefined castor sugar

a very small pinch of cream of tartar

75 g (2¾ oz) unrefined icing sugar, sifted

600 ml (1 pint) double cream, very
lightly whipped

serves 6–8

As children we were often fed malt loaf, as it was cheap and very good for you. I really like it, it's great just sliced and spread with cold butter. Malt loaf has fallen out of fashion over the past few years and is one of those foods you see all the time in the supermarket but never really know what to do with. Well, look no further, here is a fantastic dessert, quick and very moreish.

This recipe produces quite a lot but it isn't really feasible to make it in a smaller quantity (for some reason, some recipes are like this). Just make it and freeze it in two containers, it keeps fine for a month.

Put the malt loaf into a food processor and blitz to make a fine crumb – it will stick together but don't worry.

Place the egg yolks in the bowl of a food mixer. Put the castor sugar and 150 ml (¼ pint) of cold water in a pan and bring to the boil. Once boiling, leave to boil for 5 minutes exactly, no more no less – I use a small digital timer.

Once the sugar and water have been boiling for 2 minutes, set the mixer to medium speed.

After 5 minutes, take the sugar and water off the stove, turn the mixer up to full speed and pour the syrup on to the egg yolks. Continue whisking until the mixture is thick, foamy and cold.

When the egg mixture is cold, lightly whisk the egg whites with the cream of tartar, until foamy but not grainy, and then add the icing sugar and whisk well.

Remove the bowl from the machine, add the malt loaf and break up carefully with a spatula. Fold in the lightly whipped cream and, finally, the egg whites. Pour into two containers and freeze overnight or for up to two weeks. That's it, serve with biscuits or Macaroons (page 133).

caramelised croissant
parfait

2 large all-butter croissants, about 140 g
(5 oz) total weight

2.5 ml (½ teaspoon) grated nutmeg

2.5 ml (½ teaspoon) ground mixed spice

85 g (3 oz) dark brown muscovado sugar

for the meringue

4 large egg whites

75 g (2¾ oz) castor sugar

75 g (2¾ oz) light brown soft sugar

250 ml (9 fl oz) whipping cream

juice and finely grated zest of 1 lemon

This is my variation of the very famous and much copied brown bread ice cream. It came about quite by chance, because I needed to use up the all-butter croissants left over from breakfast.

Preheat the oven to 180°C/350°F/Gas Mark 4. Lightly wet a 900 g (2 lb) loaf tin and then line with cling film (the water helps you line the tin more easily).

Pop the croissants into a food processor and blitz to make fine breadcrumbs. Add the spices and muscovado sugar and blitz again very briefly, just to mix together.

Tip the crumbs on to a large baking sheet, spread out evenly and then bake for about 8–10 minutes, or until golden brown and producing a wonderful aroma – keep an eye on the crumbs as they can burn very quickly. Once browned, remove from the oven and cool.

Place the egg whites in a very clean bowl and whisk until they have a thick and creamy look to them but are not grainy (see page 129). At this point, add the castor sugar and continue to whisk on a high speed until glossy and shiny, then add the light brown sugar and whisk again until very thick, this will take about 5–6 minutes.

Whip the cream to soft peaks. Fold the whipped cream into the meringue, along with the croissant crumbs and lemon juice and zest. Spoon into the lined loaf tin and cover with a piece of cling film. Freeze overnight or for a couple of weeks.

When frozen, unwrap and cut into slices. Serve with a tart raspberry sauce.

frozen blackcurrant mousse

350 g (12 oz) blackcurrants

4 egg whites

a pinch of cream of tartar

125 g (4½ oz) golden castor sugar

250 ml (9 fl oz) double cream,
lightly whipped

serves 4–6

This is a good way of making ice cream without a machine – it's quick and easy. Make it with other summer berries, such as strawberries and raspberries, but for these you may need to reduce the sugar as they are sweeter than blackcurrants to start with.

Blitz the blackcurrants in a food processor to make a purée and then sieve to remove the pips.

Line a lightly oiled 1 kg (2 lb) loaf tin with cling film.

Next, whisk the egg whites with the cream of tartar until lightly foamy but holding their own weight. Add half the sugar and beat until firm and glossy, then add the rest of the sugar and whisk until very firm.

Fold the cream into the meringue, then add the purée and carefully fold together well, but do not over mix.

Pour the mixture into the lined loaf tin, cover with cling film and freeze overnight. Or keep in the freezer for a couple of weeks.

Unwrap and slice with a hot knife. Serve with a few summer berries and a little extra whipped double cream.

SORBETS & GRANITAS

The great chef Escoffier once wrote about sorbets: 'Sherbets and their derivative preparations consist of light, barely-congealed ices, served after the entrées, they serve in freshening the stomach; preparing it properly to receive the roast.' As an apprentice, no large meal I helped prepare would be served without the obligatory sorbet course. This custom seems to have fallen by the wayside. The only time I would contemplate serving a sorbet course now is on Christmas day, as the menu is not only very large, but also very filling!

Nowadays most sorbets are eaten as puddings or desserts, and are one of the most pleasurable things to eat and make. No dish brings out the natural perfume and flavour of ripe fruit better than a sorbet. Not only that, but you always end up with stunning colours too. Yorkshire forced rhubarb makes the best coloured sorbet by far.

Not that sorbet-making is limited to fruit and syrup however. Nowadays chefs seem to make anything into a sorbet. Chocolate, coconut, tomato, and avocado, to name just a few, are all popular and can actually be quite nice if made correctly. A lot of professional chefs frown upon savoury sorbets. I'm not too sure about this. On the one hand they can taste frankly awful, but in skilled hands they can be very interesting. My colleague Heston Blumenthal from The Fat Duck at Bray has spent a lot of time experimenting with savoury sorbets and ice cream and has come up with some really different and startling concoctions; bacon and egg ice cream is his current favourite. Escoffier would not be a happy man.

All this just goes to show what can be done once you look beyond normal ingredients. I do use tamarillos in sweet sorbets. For me they are a fruit normally associated with savoury partners like venison and duck, but sorbet really is the best and only way to use these strange fruit. Apart from tamarillos I tend to stick to more mainstream ingredients like mango, pineapple, Bramley apple and new-season rhubarb.

Quinces are a very English fruit and I cook a lot of them. They seem to have been forgotten and it's a real shame. Once used in huge amounts by medieval cooks, they are a real joy to cook with and eat. One or two of these delightful fruit placed in a bowl will perfume the whole room. The only problem is they must be gently simmered or baked to render them useable in a sorbet. Here I bake them first, which intensifies their unique flavour.

techniques

The secret with sorbet is to get the perfect balance of flavour, sweetness and dead smooth, almost fudgy consistency. Far too often sorbet is too crystalline, almost crunchy. This is due to insufficient use of sugar or glucose syrup or, in some cases, alcohol. However if you use too much syrup, the sorbet will be too sweet – it's a fine line.

Escoffier also said that, 'Fruit sorbets are generally prepared from the juices and syrups of aqueous fruits. Fruit purées are scarcely suited to this mode of procedure and they are only resorted to in exceptional cases.' What he meant, in my view, is that a fruit syrup has a wonderful perfume and clarity of flavour and that it is easy to freeze, unlike a thick, grainy purée with added sugar.

Anyway, the best tip I can give people when it comes to making sorbet is to taste, taste and keep tasting. Different fruit, chocolate and so on have different levels of sweetness, so it's hard to give an exact recipe. I have tried and tested these recipes many times and I have come up with what I think is just right, but use your common sense and judge for yourselves. If you think a recipe needs a touch more syrup then add it.

Sorbets can also be enriched with double cream, without losing their unique fruit flavour. Champagne mixed with fresh orange juice and double cream makes a surprisingly light, refreshing sorbet. Alcohol too can be used in sorbets and granitas. Gin and tonic, Campari and grapefruit and white wine all work well.

Granitas are a no-hassle type of sorbet. They can be made well in advance without an ice-cream machine and are extremely simple to do. Watermelon mixed with a little alcohol is probably my favourite. It's a wonderfully refreshing way to end a meal and to me is the only way to get the best flavour out of a watermelon without the damned seeds.

stock syrup

125 g (4½ oz) granulated sugar
60 g (2¼ oz) Staboline, Trimoline or
liquid glucose

makes

250 ml (8 fl oz)

The reason why I make stock or sugar syrup is that it gives a wonderful finished texture to any ice cream or sorbet.

The glucose helps the sugar chill in a more stable form, if you do not use glucose then the texture is grainy and the ice cream or sorbet is not velvety smooth.

There are a few commercial inverted sugars on the market, Staboline or Trimoline are two that I have used and still do, but good old-fashioned liquid glucose from chemists also does a satisfactory job. I find I have to add a little more liquid glucose to get a perfect result, just experiment and you'll soon get the knack.

Pour 150 ml (¼ pint) of cold water into a pan. Weigh the sugar out on to the tray of the scales and make a small indentation in the middle. Place the jar of liquid glucose in the microwave and heat on medium power for a few seconds or until the liquid is soft and runny. Pour the warmed liquid glucose on to the sugar, weighing out as much as you need by adding the desired weight to the weight of the sugar – this way the glucose stays on the sugar and not stuck to the scale pan, which can be a real pain.

Carefully add the sugar and liquid glucose to the water and then heat to bring to the boil. Remove from the hob, cover and allow to cool. Keep covered in the fridge, where it can be stored indefinitely.

tamarillo sorbet

6 ripe tamarillos, weighing about 600 g
(1 lb 5 oz) in total
500 ml (18 fl oz) stock syrup (opposite,
make a double quantity)
5 ml (1 teaspoon) egg white
juice of 1 large lemon

makes

1.2 litres (2 pints)

This rather unusual fruit has been around for centuries, but only in the past few years has it become not only readily available, but quite trendy. Originally from South America the tree tomato or tamarillo is now grown in East Africa and the North Island of New Zealand, to name just a couple of places. The fruit says 'eat me' when you look at it but, if you were to take a bite you would probably spit it out straight away. The flesh needs to be very ripe to be eaten, the best way to tell if a tamarillo is ready is by the colour, which turns from deep orange to deep purply crimson, and if the fruit is very soft to the touch.

Tamarillos can be poached or roasted in a hot oven, but are full of seeds; I'm not a great fan of them cooked this way. Married with rich meats such as venison, hare and game a little tamarillo purée really livens up sauces, cutting strong flavours really well. But for me, there really is only one way to enjoy them and that's in a wonderfully coloured and deeply flavoured sorbet. Just great on its own or with a little poached or fresh fruit, such as pears or apricots, and a syrup, this recipe is a little different.

Place a container in the freezer to pre-chill. Top and tail the tamarillos, then carefully pare away the skin with a sharp knife. Place the fruit in a liquidiser and add the stock syrup. Blitz until you have a thick purée but take care not to go on for too long so as to avoid splitting the seeds, as this sometimes makes the purée a little bitter.

Pour the purée into a fine strainer and push through into a bowl with a ladle. Add the egg white. (This helps to bind everything together and give a nice fudgy edge to the finished sorbet. I like to add a little egg white to all my sorbets, it really does make a difference especially to juice sorbets such as lemon or lime.)

Taste the mixture and add as much of the lemon juice as necessary. Pour into an ice-cream maker and churn according to the instructions until thick. Spoon into the pre-chilled container and store in the freezer, where it will keep well for a couple of weeks.

bramley apple
sorbet

2 large Bramley apples, weighing about
750–800 g (1 lb 10 oz–1 lb 12 oz) in
total, peeled, cored and cut into
2 cm (¾-inch) pieces
juice of 1 large lemon
2 pinches of citric acid powder
250 ml (9 fl oz) stock syrup (page 190)
½ teaspoon egg white

The unique taste of this recipe reminds me of the good old-fashioned stewed apples and custard we ate as children. My mother would always stew apples and leave them to cool, and make the custard far too early and leave that to cool also. So for years I never had hot stewed apples and custard! Even now I prefer them cold, but what a perfect combination.

Well, back to this recipe. Bramley's are a wonderful apple to cook with, contrary to some people's view, and the 'marmalade' they turn into, the technical term for the stewed apple, has a depth of flavour when stewed that no other apple seems to have. Howgate Wonder does run it a close second but, for me, Bramley's are the best for stewing.

Put a container in the freezer to pre-chill. Place the apples, lemon juice and citric acid in a pan with about 250 ml (9 fl oz) of cold water and bring to the boil. Turn down the heat and gently stew over a low heat until pulpy. You should end up with about 500 g (1 lb 2 oz) apples in total.

Remove from the heat, carefully pour into a liquidiser and blitz until smooth. Spoon into a bowl, add the stock syrup and whisk well and then leave to cool.

When cool, add the egg white and whisk well again. Strain through a fine sieve then pour into the ice-cream maker and churn until firm and frozen. Transfer to the pre-chilled container and store in the freezer, where it will keep for a couple of weeks.

mango sorbet

375 g (13 oz) fresh mango flesh
(about 2 medium, ripe mangoes,
free of skin and stone)
375 ml (13 fl oz) stock syrup (page 190),
made with 185 g (6½ oz) granulated
sugar, 225 ml (8 fl oz) water and
90 g (3¼ oz) liquid glucose
juice of 1 large lemon

serves 4–6

Made into a sorbet, mango takes on a dense, fudgy texture that no other fruit has. I'm not too sure why, but the result is fantastic.

I have tried to replicate this glorious texture in other sorbets by using all sorts of tricks, including starches and egg white, but never really attained a good result. The closest is gelatine, melted and added to white chocolate sorbet; this not only helps the texture but also helps hold the sorbet in warm weather.

For this sorbet to taste its best, you must use very ripe, perfumed mangoes, you can also add a touch of medium white wine to the purée if you want, for an extra twist of flavour.

Place a container in the freezer to pre-chill. Place the mango in the liquidiser along with the stock syrup. Blitz until smooth and then add the lemon juice. At this point, remove the jug from the liquidizer, taste the purée and see what you think; it may need a touch more lemon juice to balance the sweetness. As there are about 1300 varieties of mango all will taste slightly different, so it's good to check.

If you are happy, then churn the mixture in an ice-cream maker until frozen, thick and shiny. Transfer to the pre-chilled container and store in a freezer for a couple of weeks.

baked quince sorbet

2 medium perfumed quinces, weighing
about 600 g (1 lb 5 oz) in total
250 ml (9 fl oz) stock syrup (page 190)
juice of 2 large lemons

serves 6–8

Baked quinces take on a beautiful pinky-orange hue, it does take a little time but is well worth the wait. All the juices and flavour are kept inside the tightly wrapped foil and there is no need to skin them either, I think the skin gives the finished sorbet a nice speckled finish. I also like to bake quinces, scoop out the tough, grainy centres and serve then warm with clotted cream and a sprinkling of nutmeg or cinnamon.

Most supermarkets and grocers will start to stock quinces by late September and they are still around in late January, though by then they are imported from Turkey and Iran.

Preheat the oven to 200°C/400°F/Gas Mark 6. Wrap the quinces in two layers of foil and place on a baking sheet. Pop in the oven and cook for about 1 hour. The reason I'm a bit vague here is that, having cooked this recipe four times, I have concluded that all quinces cook at different times. So I took the average of the four and it came out at about an hour; just use your common sense, when the quinces are cooked there should be no resistance at all when they are squeezed. When ready, leave to cool completely.

Place an empty container in the freezer to chill. Cut the quinces in half and remove the grainy, tough core. Place the fruit in a liquidiser and add the stock syrup and lemon juice. Blitz until smooth and transfer straight into the ice-cream machine.

Churn until frozen – this will take about 15–20 minutes – then transfer to the pre-chilled container and store in the freezer, where it will keep for a couple of weeks.

pink champagne sorbet

with double cream

375 ml (13 fl oz) pink Champagne

375 ml (13 fl oz) freshly squeezed
orange juice, strained

375 ml (13 fl oz) stock syrup (page 190),
made with 185 g (6½ oz) granulated
sugar, 225 ml (8 fl oz) water and 90 g
(3¼ oz) liquid glucose

juice of 2 lemons

brandy

400 ml (14 fl oz) double cream,
lightly whipped

makes

about 1.5 litres (2¾ pints)

Most people think of sorbets as made with just water, flavouring and sugar. Well, that's right as far as it goes but you can also add a twist to sorbets by including cream, which makes the texture smooth, creamy and silky. Here is a very clever recipe from a chap called Allan Garth, a chef I used to work for years ago. It's very simple and very refreshing and a great way to end a heavy meal.

I like to serve coconut biscuits or Brandy Snaps (page 291) with this sorbet.

Place a container in the freezer to pre-chill. Pour the Champagne, orange juice, stock syrup, lemon juice and a dash of brandy into a bowl and whisk together. Churn the mixture in an ice-cream maker until thick and frozen or just freeze until thick and slushy.

Remove the mixture from the machine and place in a cold bowl. Add the whipped cream and whisk together – the mixture might turn lumpy but that's quite normal. Spoon into the pre-chilled container, seal the lid and freeze overnight; any lumps will disappear. You can keep it in the freezer for a couple of weeks.

Scoop the sorbet out and serve in glasses, with coconut biscuits.

white chocolate sorbet

30 ml (2 tablespoons) liquid glucose

125 g (4½ oz) castor sugar

1 gelatine leaf, soaked in cold water

225 ml (8 fl oz) single cream

175 g (6 oz) good-quality white chocolate, melted

This sorbet does sound a little odd but it is very refreshing eaten on its own or with Bitter Chocolate Tart (page 84).

Place a container in the freezer to pre-chill. Heat the liquid glucose, sugar and 450 ml (16 fl oz) of cold water together in a pan until dissolved.

Remove from the heat and add the gelatine, stirring until dissolved. Cool slightly.

Finally, add the single cream and melted chocolate and whisk well. Cool until the liquid is at room temperature and then churn in an ice-cream maker until thick and creamy.

Transfer the mixture to the chilled container and store in the freezer for up to two weeks.

creamy coconut sorbet

200 g (7 oz) block of creamed coconut,
cut into small cubes
300 ml (½ pint) boiling water
250 ml (9 fl oz) stock syrup (page 190)
100 ml (3½ fl oz) Malibu liqueur
100 ml (3½ fl oz) single cream
15 ml (1 tablespoon) egg white

This is a little different from the normal smooth sorbets. I think it's sometimes nice to ring the changes and this sorbet has a nice coconutty, grainy texture. This is a deliciously rich accompaniment to Coconut Tart or Bitter Chocolate Tart (pages 62 and 84). It's also very good with fresh fruit.

Leave a container in the freezer to pre-chill. Place the creamed coconut in a heatproof bowl, pour over the boiling water and stir until dissolved. Leave to cool.

Mix together the cooled coconut cream, stock syrup, Malibu, cream and egg white. Pour into the ice-cream maker and churn until smooth and frozen. Transfer to the pre-chilled container and store in the freezer for a couple of weeks.

fresh pineapple sorbet

500 g (1 lb 2 oz) cored, skinned sweet
pineapple (prepared weight),
roughly chopped
250 ml (9 fl oz) stock syrup (page 190)
a pinch of citric acid
5 ml (1 teaspoon) egg white

serves 4–6

The two points to remember about this sorbet are to use ripe, sweet pineapples to get a satisfactory result (Del Monte brand is usually reliable), and make sure to liquidise very well, or the finished sorbet will have a grainy texture.

Place a container in the freezer to pre-chill. Place the pineapple, syrup and citric acid in a liquidiser and blitz until very smooth. Pour into a bowl and whisk in the egg white.

Transfer to an ice-cream maker and churn until thick and frozen. Spoon into the pre-chilled container and store in the freezer for a couple of weeks.

watermelon granita

350 ml (12 fl oz) white sweet dessert wine

45 ml (3 tablespoons) liquid glucose

120 g (4¼ oz) castor sugar

1 watermelon, weighing about 3 kg
(6 lb 8 oz)

juice of 1 lemon

serves 4

Watermelon is one of those fruits that look and taste wonderful but is a real pain to eat – those blessed pips are very annoying. Here you get all the flavour without the pips.

Place a container in the freezer to pre-chill. Place the wine, glucose and sugar in a stainless-steel saucepan and dissolve over a low heat. The glucose gives a soft crystalline finish to the granita.

Cut the watermelon in half. Scoop the flesh out of one of the halves and place it in a food processor. Blitz and then pass through a sieve to remove all the pips. Measure the purée, you should end up with about 600 ml (1 pint). If there is not enough, process a little more watermelon or top up with a little cold water.

Stir the melon purée and lemon juice into the white-wine syrup, pour into the pre-chilled container and freeze overnight or keep it in the freezer for a week.

Cut the remaining melon into wedges or chunks.

Remove the granita from the freezer, scrape off the top layer with a spoon or spatula, so you end up with a pile of fine crystals. Serve straight away, in a glass bowl with the remaining fresh watermelon.

new-season rhubarb sorbet

650 g (1 lb 7 oz) new-season rhubarb,
cut into 2 cm (¾-inch) pieces
225 g (8 oz) unrefined castor sugar
juice of 1 large lemon
180 g (6¼ oz) liquid glucose

This beautifully coloured sorbet is probably one of my favourites. New-season rhubarb is perfect for sorbets, poaching or oven-baking. It's only around for a few short weeks in the early part of the year so make the most of it. It will freeze well if blanched first, but I like to bottle mine in a light syrup.

The good thing about this recipe is that everything can be cooked together in one pan, liquidise and then churn in an ice-cream maker.

Put a container in the freezer to pre-chill. Place all the ingredients in a pan, mix well and gently heat until the sugar starts to melt. Turn up the heat until the fruit simmers and then cook with the lid on (this keeps all the moisture in the pan) for about 10 minutes or until the fruit is nicely puréed.

Spoon into a liquidiser and blitz until you have a very fine purée. Leave to cool.

Spoon into the ice-cream maker and churn until thick and frozen. Transfer to the pre-chilled container and store in the freezer for up to two weeks.

white wine granita
with blood oranges

8 blood oranges

for the granita
115 g (4 oz) castor sugar
30 ml (2 tablespoons) liquid glucose
350 ml (12 fl oz) dry white wine
juice of 1 lemon and 1 lime

serves 4

Blood oranges always fascinated me as a child: they had such a beautiful colour and were only around for such a short time. Apart from mandarins, these are by far the finest dessert oranges. The two most common varieties are Moro and Tarocco and Sicily remains the best area for growing these heavenly little oranges.

The redness is due to a combination of cold nights and mild sunny days, which causes a chemical reaction in the skin.

Blood oranges themselves make a great sorbet and the juice combines very well with a little butter and fish stock to make the most sublime sauce to serve with roasted scallops.

Put a container in the freezer to pre-chill. Place the sugar, glucose and 300 ml (½ pint) of cold water in a stainless steel saucepan and dissolve over a low heat. (The glucose gives a crystalline finish to the granita.) Stir in the wine and lime and lemon juice and transfer to the container. Freeze overnight or for up to a week.

When ready to serve, peel and segment the oranges, removing every bit of pith and all the pips and reserving any juice that comes out. Pile the segments into four bowls.

Remove the granita from the freezer and scrape off the top layer with a spatula, so you end up with a pile of fine crystals. Pile on top of the segments and add a little blood orange juice. Serve straight away.

QUICK PUDDINGS

I love quick puddings. They are a great way of getting a hit of sugar with the minimum of fuss. All the puds in this chapter are extremely simple and rely on ingredients that are widely available in a supermarket. It's amazing what you can achieve with a few bits and bobs and a little thought.

Knickerbocker Glory is an anything-goes recipe — just as long as you include huge amounts of ice cream, chocolate sauce, sponge and lashings of cream. Another favourite, along the same lines, is Banana Split. As kids, we sometimes ate at a restaurant in Dover called The Britannia. It was a real treat. All the greats were on the menu: prawn cocktail with a tomato rose, steak au poivre (cooked at the table of course) and Chicken

Maryland, to name but a few. The dessert course was the best bit — Banana Split in all its glory. I can still recall looking forward to the pudding so much that by the time it arrived it was almost an anticlimax. I remember the shape of the thick glass dish, and the two long-handled spoons were great fun. Nowadays Banana Split is frowned upon. I think that's a bit sad, so I've set to work re-inventing this classic.

A lot of these puds involve cooking fruit very quickly and adding a little cream and sugar. I have cooked the sautéed pears and apples in Calvados for some 20 years. It's always quick, easy and very tasty. More up to date are the plums on toast, the Muscat grapes and the fresh pineapple with chilli syrup.

Another favourite of mine is Eton Mess. It's a great recipe but trendy chefs and food writers play around with it too much. The same could be said about jellies. I like jelly very much provided it's very lightly set and full of flavour. I've eaten some pretty awful examples recently.

No quick puddings section would be complete without Angel Cake in there somewhere. The soft, crumbly, delicate sponge with its pastel colours is probably the most vivid of all my childhood memories. It can be used as a base for trifle instead of swiss roll (most swiss rolls, I'm afraid, don't taste like the old-fashioned ones used to). Nowadays I top Angel Cake with fresh raspberries and Bird's custard as a quick pud for the kids and they love it.

see also

hot and cold chocolate milk shake with
cookies *page 94*

knickerbocker glory

4 × 1 cm (½-inch) slices of swiss roll,
cut into small pieces

2 scoops of fudge ice cream

55 g (2 oz) chopped walnuts

Bitter Chocolate Sauce (page 243) or
good-quality ready-made chocolate sauce

Raspberry Sauce (page 246)

4 scoops of good-quality vanilla ice cream

very lightly whipped double cream

a few 'cigarette' biscuits

serves 2

There are so many varieties of this sweet that there really is no set format. You just need ice cream, raspberry sauce, chocolate sauce, chopped nuts, whipped double cream and swiss roll. Vanilla ice cream is the best, perhaps with a touch of, say, fudge, to add a little extra twist.

The only way to serve this is in very tall glasses with very long spoons. This is fun and makes the whole eating experience even nicer.

Place some of the chopped swiss roll in the bottoms of two sundae glasses. Add a ball of fudge ice cream to each.

Sprinkle over a few nuts and a generous slug each of raspberry and chocolate sauce.

Add the rest of the sponge and two balls of vanilla ice cream to each glass.

Finally top with whipped cream, more nuts and the rest of the two sauces. Pop in the cigarette biscuits and get stuck in! It really is as easy as that.

banana splits

125 g (4½ oz) granulated sugar

12 pecan or walnut halves

250 ml (8 fl oz) whipping cream, whipped

4 brandy-snap baskets (optional)

Raspberry Sauce (page 246)

8 scoops of good-quality vanilla ice cream

8 apple bananas

Bitter Chocolate Sauce (page 243)

icing sugar, to decorate

serves 4

A classic pudding. In the late sixties and seventies the banana split was the dessert to have in posh restaurants, sadly it has become a bit of a joke, which I think is unfair because its combination of flavours and textures is very well balanced. Forget the calories and enjoy it!

If you don't want to use brandy-snap baskets, just serve in a dessert glass. Apple bananas are baby bananas the size of a small courgette, with a faintly ripe apple flavour. Ordinary bananas work just as well, of course.

Place the granulated sugar in a thick-bottomed pan, add 45 ml (3 tablespoons) of water and heat to dissolve the sugar; then bring to the boil (see page 171). Cook until the caramel starts to turn a pale golden-brown colour; then remove from the heat and drop in the nuts. Swirl around and then, using a fork, lift out the nuts one at a time and place on baking parchment or greased greaseproof paper. Leave to cool completely.

To serve, place a small blob of whipped cream on a plate and top with a brandy-snap basket, if you are using them. Spoon a little of the raspberry sauce around the biscuit and then scoop two balls of ice cream into the basket (be careful as the biscuits are very delicate). Cut the bananas in half lengthways and divide between the baskets. Decorate with more whipped cream, caramel nut halves and a light drizzle of chocolate sauce. Dust with icing sugar and serve straight away.

muscat grapes
warmed in vanilla butter and lemon oil

400 ml (14 fl oz) Sauvignon Blanc

100 g (3½ oz) castor sugar

2 vanilla pods, split

50 g (1¾ oz) unsalted butter

5 ml (1 teaspoon) lemon oil

400 g (14 oz) muscat grapes

serves 4

A very simple and tasty dessert. Just bear in mind that the sweetness of the grapes may vary so, before you start weighing out the bits and bobs, taste the grapes, and adjust the sugar content accordingly. You should then be able to judge the amount of sugar needed more accurately.

Put the wine, sugar, vanilla seeds and pods and butter into a saucepan and bring to the boil. Reduce until the butter emulsifies with the wine and sugar.

Add the oil and grapes and just warm through.

Serve in small bowls and top each with half of one of the vanilla pod. You will not need very much of this pudding as it's very rich.

hot plums
on toast

25 g (1 oz) unsalted butter

25 g (1 oz) soft light brown sugar

juice of ½ lime

1 thick slice of bread, from crust end

3 Victoria plums, halved and stoned

serves 1

A different way to eat plums – the secret is to use the crust from the loaf and to leave the juices to soak into the bread once cooked. I use Victoria plums for this dish as they are slightly firmer and less sweet than ruby red ones.

Preheat the oven to 220°C/425°F/Gas Mark 7. Gently heat the butter and sugar together in a pan until melted and then increase the heat and bring to the boil. Add the lime juice, remove from the heat and stir well.

Sit the crust of bread on a baking sheet and arrange the plums on top. Spoon over half the lime and butter mixture and then place the tray in the oven and bake for 10 minutes. After this time, spoon over the rest of the mixture and cook for a further 10 minutes or until the plums are just soft and the bread is browning nicely.

Remove from the oven and allow to cool for 5 minutes. Carefully lift the plum toast off the tray using a fish slice and serve at once.

warm pears
with almonds and vanilla sugar

4 ripe Williams, Red Bartlett or Comice pears

40 g (1½ oz) unsalted butter

1 vanilla pod, split

about 55 g (2 oz) castor sugar

finely grated zest and juice of 1 large orange

about 300 ml (½ pint) double cream

15 ml (1 tablespoon) finely chopped fresh mint

40 g (1½ oz) flaked almonds, lightly browned in a hot oven

serves 4

Pears are a very versatile fruit, in Britain alone there are something like 100 varieties, and apparently about 6000 varieties grown worldwide, although you only really see a couple of dozen or so used these days.

By the sixteenth century there were nearly 250 varieties available in Italy, and 1500 in America alone. Today, though, you will see only the occasional unusual variety – and I have to say that the supermarkets have done their bit here, in trying to get people to buy an alternative to the familiar ones you see day in day out. Good ones for this dish include Comice, Red Bartlett and Williams Bon Chretien. Do look out for Anjou, a very juicy variety, and Packham's Triumph, with sweet succulent flesh.

With this recipe, do taste the fruit first and then adjust the amount of sugar to taste: there is nothing worse than an over sweet dish.

Remove the base from the pears, then carefully remove the skin with a sharp vegetable peeler, trying to keep to the natural shape of the pear. Cut each pear into six pieces and remove the core and seeds.

Heat the butter in a sauté or deep frying pan until it starts to foam. Scrape in the seeds from the vanilla pod, add the pod and sugar and then add the pears and gently brown in the butter on all sides.

Add the orange zest and juice and cook for 15–20 seconds, then pour in the cream and warm through; the cream will thicken straight away. Do not overcook the pears or they will disintegrate. Just as the cream and juice is simmering, remove from the heat and add the chopped mint. Taste and adjust if necessary by adding more sugar or orange juice.

Spoon into warm bowls and sprinkle over the almonds. You can increase the amount of cream you use if you want to; I like the nice balance of this amount.

sautéed apples
in calvados

4 large Cox's apples

55 g (2 oz) unsalted butter

20 ml (4 teaspoons) castor sugar

200 ml (7 fl oz) Calvados

60 ml (4 tablespoons) double cream

30 ml (2 tablespoons) chopped fresh
lemon balm or mint

serves 4

There are about 250 varieties of apple in Britain today. A lot of once out of favour, older varieties are now being grown again, which is good to see: George Cave, a crimson blush with sweet flesh, Laxton's Superb, with a yellow skin and deep sweet flavour that is great with cheese and Howgate Wonder, the best baking apple by far, are all being sold again and about time.

I use a lot of Granny Smith apples in my cooking: they are a tart, firm apple that can stand up to all sorts of harsh treatment – whether it's being plunged into caramel, baked in a pie or even roasted in the oven a Granny Smith will fare well. Cox's are not only a superb eating apple but a great apple to cook lightly, or even to pickle, and hardly need any sugar at all. The only thing to take care with is not to lose the wonderful aroma that the Cox has by overcooking it.

This pudding is a real favourite of mine and a great light ending to the meal.

Top and tail the apples and cut into quarters. Carefully remove the skin with a small paring knife and then cut each quarter into three or four thin slices. You will have to work quickly so the apples do not turn brown; remember that you cannot put them into water or add lemon juice to them or they will not brown in the butter.

Heat a large non-stick sauté or frying pan. Add the butter and, once it starts to foam, add the apples and sugar and toss around so they colour slightly; do not overcook.

Pour in the Calvados – be aware that once the Calvados is hot it may ignite straight away so do take care, it looks good on the telly but believe me it can come as quite a shock. If it does ignite then do not panic, it will soon burn off.

Add the double cream and swirl around until fully incorporated and then cook until the apples are cooked but still have slight bite to them; do take care as they will turn into mush very quickly indeed. Finally pop in the chopped lemon balm or mint. Serve in deep bowls.

sautéed bananas

with brown sugar, lime and cream

15 g (½ oz) unsalted butter

2 large, ripe bananas, cut into 2 cm (¾-inch) chunks

55 g (2 oz) soft brown sugar

juice and finely grated zest of 1 lime

60 ml (4 tablespoons) double cream

serves 2

Heat a wok or large frying pan, add the butter and heat until it just begins to foam and turn a 'nutty' brown colour. Pop in the bananas and stir around to coat in butter; sprinkle over the sugar and continue to cook for about 30 seconds (do not overcook).

Add the lime juice and zest, spoon the banana mixture into two bowls and drizzle over the cream.

grilled figs
with mulled wine sauce and sabayon

8 fresh, ripe figs

for the sauce

600 ml (1 pint) full-bodied red wine

1 cinnamon stick

6 cloves

2.5 ml (½ teaspoon) freshly grated nutmeg

115 g (4 oz) castor sugar plus 40 ml
(8 teaspoons)

1 vanilla pod, split

finely grated zest and juice of 1 lemon
and 1 orange

40 g (1½ oz) cold unsalted butter, cubed

for the sabayon

3 large egg yolks

55 g (2 oz) castor sugar

50 ml (2 fl oz) white wine

serves 4

A strange combination but a very nice one. The secret is to use very ripe figs and just warm them through under a hot grill; do not overheat them or they will fall apart.

To make the sauce, place the wine, cinnamon, cloves, nutmeg, 115 g (4 oz) castor sugar, vanilla pod and lemon and orange zest and juice in a stainless-steel saucepan and reduce by two-thirds.

Whisk in the cold butter, cover and keep the sauce warm but not hot.

Preheat the grill. Cut the figs in half lengthways and sprinkle 2.5 ml (½ teaspoon) castor sugar on to each half. Place under the hot grill and warm through for a maximum of 2–3 minutes.

Meanwhile, place the sabayon ingredients in a bowl, and whisk over a pan of gently simmering water until thick and foamy.

To serve, place four fig halves in a bowl and drizzle over a little red wine sauce. Top with a spoon of the sabayon froth and eat straight away.

fresh pineapple
with chilli and vanilla syrup

115 g (4 oz) castor sugar

1 vanilla pod, split

1 small red chilli, de-seeded and finely chopped

about 55 g (2 oz) unsalted butter

1 fresh, medium pineapple, peeled and cut in 1 cm (½-inch) slices

serves 4

Place 100 ml (3½ fl oz) of cold water and the sugar in a small saucepan, along with the vanilla pod and chilli, and bring to the boil. Once the syrup has come to the boil, take it off the heat immediately and leave to infuse and cool for about 30 minutes or until just cool to the touch.

Heat a non-stick frying pan and melt the butter. Just as the butter stops foaming and is about to turn brown, pop in the pineapple slices and brown on both sides, this should take a few minutes. Once they are slightly browned, add the chilli syrup and bring to the boil (the butter will slightly thicken the syrup).

Serve straight away, either warm or hot but never cold. It's rather nice to accompany this dish with some greek-style yogurt to offset the sweetness of the whole pudding.

iced charentais melon
with beaumes de venise sabayon

2 ripe and well perfumed Charentais melons

15 ml (1 tablespoon) finely chopped fresh
lemon balm or verbena

1 quantity Beaumes de Venise Sabayon
(page 239)

4–8 pieces of My Mum's Shortbread
(page 298), to serve

serves 4

Very simple and very easy. The secret is to make sure the melon is as cold as possible, so the contrast between the two, warm and cold, makes the mouth come alive. This recipe is pictured on page 238.

Cut the melon in half. Carefully scoop out the melon flesh using a parisienne scoop or a teaspoon, making sure that you get as much as possible of the fruit itself out (I'm not that bothered if you end up with a few half balls, it's more important to use as much of the sweet flesh as possible).

Add the lemon balm or verbena and mix well and then chill so it is really cold – a good 2–3 hours is best.

Spoon the melon balls into tall glasses and then straight away spoon over the Beaumes de Venise sabayon and serve with shortbread. This is possibly the nicest summer dessert ever.

passion-fruit jelly
with shortbread

3 gelatine leaves

8 passion-fruit

fresh orange juice (must be fresh), strained

about 115 g (4 oz) castor sugar

8 fingers of My Mum's Shortbread

(page 298), to serve

serves 4

Passion-fruit basically fall into two categories, ripe and unripe. This small, intensely flavoured fruit is firm, and slightly green in appearance when under ripe, and when ripe starts to shrivel and loose its green hue. I prefer to use the fruit when they are older, you seem to get more juice out, and, the juice seems to be slightly sweeter.

A little juice from this fruit goes a long way and can overpower a dish very easily, so I add fresh orange juice to the passion-fruit to get a better balance.

Soak the leaf gelatine in a little cold water until soft and pliable (see page 99). Make sure the gelatine is soaked very well indeed: the smallest amount of un-soaked gelatine in the finished jelly is awful.

Cut the passion-fruit in half and remove all the seeds and juice with a teaspoon. Place in a food processor, not a liquidiser, which would purée the pips as well, leaving you with a black-speckled end product. Using a food processor on the pulse button will take the flesh from the seeds perfectly. Sieve the seeds and juice and take care to extract every last drop. Place the sieved juice in a measuring jug and top up to the 600 ml (1 pint) mark with fresh orange juice.

Place the gelatine in a small saucepan with a little of the juice mixture and melt gently over a low heat.

Add castor sugar to taste to the juice (I've suggested 115 g/4 oz as a guideline, but taste and adjust to your own preference). Stir until dissolved; it's a bit of a pain but as we want to keep the taste as fresh as possible you should not warm any of the juice at all.

Add the dissolved gelatine to the juice, stir well and pour into a bowl to set. Chill well, preferably overnight.

To serve, lightly break up with a spoon and spoon into tall glasses. Serve with shortbread and clotted cream.

dry cider and perry
jelly

300 ml (½ pint) dry cider

115 g (4 oz) castor sugar

3 gelatine leaves, soaked in cold water
(see page 99)

300 ml (½ pint) perry

1 Charles Ross apple

1 Russet apple

1 small, ripe mango

juice of ½ lemon

a few autumn raspberries (optional)

serves 4–6

A very simple and unusual dessert. I use perry, a traditional drink made from pears, with cider to give a very refreshing adult jelly.

It's also very nice to use two varieties of apple that are not normally spoken about, but which are now available in the supermarkets. They are slightly more expensive but well worth the extra cost.

Pour the cider and sugar into a pan, heat until the sugar has dissolved and then bring to the boil. Remove from the heat and add the soaked gelatine.

Once the gelatine has melted, add the perry and mix together, then pour into a shallow dish and allow to cool slightly.

Peel and core the apples and peel the mango. Cut the fruit into small pieces and stir into the cooled cider and perry. Finally, add the lemon juice and raspberries, if using, and stir well. Cover with cling film and chill until set.

It's best to break the jelly up slightly before you serve it, so the fruit is dispersed when eaten. Spoon into glasses and top with a little clotted cream.

blackberry, porridge
and honey yogurt

140 g (5 oz) cooled, cooked porridge (made
with no salt), broken up with a fork
100 g (3½ oz) Jordan's Original cereal
400 g (14 oz) sheep's milk yogurt
350 g (12 oz) fresh, very ripe blackberries
finely grated zest and juice of 1 lime
85 g (3 oz) unrefined castor sugar
60 ml (4 tablespoons) runny honey

serves 4–6

Great way to use up cold porridge, this really is very refreshing and any summer fruit will do just as well as blackberries. Just try it!

Mix together the porridge, cereal and yogurt.

Place the blackberries, lime juice and zest and castor sugar in a separate bowl then gently crush with a potato masher to break up the fruit very slightly.

Carefully fold the blackberries into the porridge, so you end up with a 'ripple' effect.

Spoon into wide glasses or bowls, layering with honey. Chill for at least and hour and preferably overnight.

angel cake
with raspberries, mango and custard

200 g can of mango slices, drained
1 angel cake, cut into 4 chunks
small punnet of fresh raspberries
two 150 g tubs of low-fat custard
sprinkles or silver balls, to decorate

serves 4 children

All kids love the taste and texture of angel cake. I adored it as a child. Here we surreptitiously add a little fruit in the way of canned mango. Fresh mangoes are fine, but a little expensive and sometimes not too ripe, so I always keep a can in the cupboard. You could also use leftover Saffron Cake (page 270), Chocolate Cup Cakes (page 95), Glazed Chocolate Cake (page 96) or Baby Bakewells (page 281) for this idea

Divide the mango slices between four small bowls. Top each with a piece of sponge and then sprinkle over a few raspberries. Finally, spoon over the cold custard and dot with a few 'sprinkles' or silver balls. Who said kids' food is not delicious?

sweet spiced naan bread
with yogurt and oranges

finely grated zest of 1 lime

10 ml (2 teaspoons) green cardamom pods

1.25 ml (½ teaspoon) ground cloves

1 vanilla pod, seeds removed and pod
roughly chopped

115 g (4 oz) unsalted butter, softened

115 g (4 oz) unrefined dark
muscovado sugar

2 large plain naan breads, about 150 g
(5½ oz) each

greek-style yogurt and orange segments,
to serve

serves 4

A great idea, different and unusual, try it with all sorts of spices. The thicker greek-style yogurt is best for this dish; if not available use a sheep's milk yogurt.

Preheat the oven to 180°C/350°F Gas Mark 4. Place the lime zest, cardamom, cloves and vanilla seeds and pod in a spice grinder and blitz until smooth. (If you don't have a spice grinder, use the food processor or grind the spices with a rolling pin.) Tip into a bowl, add the butter and sugar and mix well.

Carefully slice the top layer off the top of the naan bread to reveal the spongy inside.

Spread the spice and butter mixture right to the edges.

Place on a non-stick baking sheet and bake for about 10 minutes, or until nicely browned. Remove from the oven and leave to cool and crispen.

Cut into slices and serve with yogurt and orange segments.

lavender shortbread
with strawberries and fromage frais

450 g (1 lb) small English strawberries

400 g (14 oz) fromage frais

juice of ½ lime

unrefined icing sugar, sifted

Lavender Shortbread (page 293)

serves 4

I started experimenting with lavender when we started growing our own and I discovered how wonderful the smell is when fresh. I started to play around with the flavour and found that the combination of strawberries, lavender and a very crumbly biscuit is a very good one indeed.

Hull and halve the strawberries and place in a large bowl.

Spoon the fromage frais into another bowl, add the lime juice and sweeten to taste with icing sugar.

Put the lavender shortbread on a plate. Now just put all three items on the table and let people tuck in and help themselves.

pancakes
with bottled blueberries

for the pancakes

2 eggs

100 g (3½ oz) plain white flour

a pinch of salt

a pinch of sugar

about 75 ml (2½ fl oz) whole milk

15 ml (1 tablespoon) vegetable oil

for the filling

500 ml (18 fl oz) whole milk

4 egg yolks

150 g (5½ oz) castor sugar

75 g (3½ oz) plain white flour

finely grated zest of 1 lime

225 g (8 oz) bottled blueberries, drained well

for the sabayon

2 egg yolks

50 g (1¾ oz) castor sugar

60 ml (4 tablespoons) white wine

serves 4

This is a nice way of serving pancakes and using bottled blueberries gives an interesting edge. My dear grandmother used to cook with the fresh berries picked by myself and my two brothers in the Trough of Bowland in Lancashire. I believe you could buy the dried variety produced in Poland, on Blackburn market some years ago. If anyone knows where to get them now, please let me know as I am desperate to find out if they are still around. They could be reconstituted and used for this recipe very satisfactorily. Bottled blueberries are hard to make at home so just buy a good-quality brand from the supermarket.

First make the pancakes. Place the eggs in a bowl with the flour, salt, sugar and half the milk and whisk well. Gradually add the rest of the milk and whisk until you have a smooth batter.

Heat the vegetable oil in a 24 cm (9½-inch) non-stick pan until just smoking. Pour in 4–5 tablespoons of the batter and swirl around until you have covered the bottom of the pan, don't worry too much about any small holes. Cook for a minute or until just set, then flip over and brown the other side for 30 seconds. Turn out on to a plate, reheat the pan and continue the process until you have four pancakes.

To make the filling, bring the milk to the boil. Whisk the egg yolks and sugar together until thick and creamy. Add the flour and mix well. Pour on the boiling milk and whisk well. Return to the pan and cook over a low heat, stirring continuously, until thick and set. Add the lime zest and pour into a bowl. Cover with cling film and allow to cool.

When you come to serve, spoon half the drained blueberries into a bowl. Add the set pastry cream and carefully fold together.

Spoon a quarter of the mixture into the centre of a pancake. Fold over the two sides and then the bottom. Finally flip over on to itself, so you end up with a small parcel. Repeat the process with the other pancakes.

Place the parcels in warmed bowls and just warm through in a moderate oven, or gently warm one at a time in the microwave. If you're using the oven, cover the bowls with foil.

Meanwhile, make the sabayon. Put all the ingredients in a heatproof bowl, place over a pan of gently simmering water and whisk until thick and foamy. Spoon some of the sabayon over each pancake and glaze with a blowtorch if you want to. Serve with the remaining berries.

pecan waffles
with strawberry jam and clotted cream

115 g (4 oz) self-raising white flour

15 g (½ oz) castor sugar

a pinch of salt

2 large eggs, separated

55 g (2 oz) pecan nuts, chopped

150–170 ml (5–6 fl oz) cold whole milk

55 g (2 oz) unsalted butter, melted

to serve

clotted cream

good-quality strawberry jam

serves 4

As a child, the only place I had waffles was on Blackpool Pleasure beach; we were allowed an ice cream or a waffle. Ever since then I have adored them. Here I'm making pecan waffles but they are equally nice plain. They are also extremely good American-style, with crisp bacon and maple syrup, and there hundreds of other variations and flavours to try.

Waffles are very simple to make provided you have a waffle iron (expensive but worth it).

Place the flour, sugar, salt, egg yolks and pecans in a bowl. Mix well, add 150 ml (¼ pint) of the milk and then a touch more if the mixture is too tight. Finally, mix in the butter.

Whisk the egg whites until they are firm (see page 129) and fold into the flour and yolk mixture. Spoon 2–3 tablespoons of the mixture into the hot iron, pull down the lid and cook for about 1 minute. Serve with lashings of clotted cream and strawberry jam.

eton mess
with rose-petal sauce

2 roses with a nice perfume

juice of 1 large lemon

heaped 30 ml (2 tablespoons) icing sugar

250 g (9 oz) English strawberries

1 vanilla pod, split, seeds removed and saved,
or a few drops of vanilla extract

15 ml (1 tablespoon) castor sugar

450 ml (16 fl oz) double cream,
very lightly whipped

4 small meringues or meringue nests,
crushed but not too small

serves 4–6

This is a classic pudding, simple, but with a nice twist; the addition of a rose-petal sauce lifts the whole thing. Meringues made with brown sugar are good, as they add a nice caramel edge to the finished sweet. It's essential that the cream is only lightly whipped or the dish will spoil.

Pick the rose petals from the stalks. Roughly chop the petals and then add the lemon juice and icing sugar and leave for 1 hour. Liquidise or whisk well so you end up with a nice chunky purée.

Meanwhile, hull the strawberries, cut into quarters and place in a bowl. Split the vanilla pod, extract the seeds and sprinkle them on the strawberries (or sprinkle over the vanilla extract), with the castor sugar and leave for 15 minutes.

To serve, fold the strawberries into the cream and then add the meringues and a little of the rose-petal sauce – do not overwork as the lemon juice will thicken the cream. Spoon into glasses and serve straight away and as cold as possible.

SABAYONS, SAUCES & FROSTINGS

A lot of the time a great pudding or cake has one or two key elements that make the finished product sensational. Carrot cake without the fresh orange and cream cheese frosting is very dry and a bit boring. Twice-baked toffee sponge without toffee sauce is very nice – but add the sauce, and a little vanilla ice cream, and even a spoonful of thick double cream and you have one of the best puddings in the world. The addition of a light, buttery shortbread biscuit and a couple of spoonfuls of a fresh, heavily-scented rose-petal syrup or a lightly perfumed saffron syrup makes all the difference to almond blancmange, believe me. And finally and this is the only exception to my rule of eating all fruit at room temperature – nothing could be nicer than very cold, beautifully ripe melon with a warm Beaumes de Venise sabayon on a hot summer's day.

Thinking up new and successful combinations of ingredients is very difficult. This is where the skill of a professional chef comes in. Having said that, even chefs get it wrong. I think the great chef Nico once said that if you can come up with one new, perfected dish per year you are doing well. Certain combinations work very well indeed and stand the test of time: chocolate and poached pear; poached peaches with fresh raspberry sauce and vanilla ice cream; coffee and walnut; orange and bitter chocolate; chocolate and mint; almonds and meringue; pavlova with passion-fruit. There are a few new additions of mine to that list that I think are real crackers: cider sabayon with warm apple puddings; fresh rose-petal syrup with blancmange; and lime water icing with baby bakewells.

All the recipes in this section are basically additions to spoon over, serve with or spread on a cake or pudding.

They range from very light, perfumed sabayons for poached fruits and hot puddings to cake coverings and frostings.

Custards are a personal favourite of mine. I sometimes add flavourings such as maple syrup to good old-fashioned custard powder that I was brought up on and also to fresh custard made with fresh eggs and vanilla. Incidentally Bird's Custard Powder was invented by the industrial chemist, Alfred Bird, in 1837 because his wife was egg intolerant. What a nice chap! And it's been a real favourite ever since. He also invented baking powder, because his wife couldn't eat yeast either.

Syrups have always been a firm favourite with the British. The Victorians and Edwardians loved to make all sorts of concoctions. A lot of the cordials you see around now started many years ago. Syrups were not only made to preserve fruit juice, they were also turned into jellies and sherbets. Escoffier used syrups for his sorbets, dismissing fruit purées. Rosehips (the fruit of the wild dog rose) were picked in huge amounts in the war years and turned into syrup to

be fed to babies and children. I could never understand why until I found out that these little hips are packed with vitamin C – about ten times as much as lemons!

Various cake coverings are also touched on. I cooked after all these years a buttercream recipe that I made in college. Buttercream was all the rage 30 years ago but seems to have fallen out of favour due to its fat content – unfairly I think. I had actually forgotten how nice it was and I've adapted the recipe for this book. Just remember the golden rule: it's not what you eat...it's how much!

see also

blackcurrant sauce *page 48*

chocolate fudge sauce *page 82*

grapefruit tea butter sauce *page 165*

mulled wine sauce *page 215*

rose-petal sauce *page 227*

cream cheese and orange frosting
page 260

flavoured syrups

225 ml (8 fl oz) cold water
30 ml (2 tablespoons) liquid glucose
200 g (7 oz) castor sugar
juice of ½ lemon

Here are a selection of ideas that I think work very well. In each case, the syrup is made with the same ingredients but each variation tells you how and when to add the different flavourings. Many other flavoured syrups are good: try a few of your own combinations.

Place the water, glucose and sugar in a pan and bring to the boil. Remove from the heat, cover and allow to cool. Finally, add lemon juice to taste to the cooled syrup (some flavours, rhubarb for instance, need a little less acidity).

cardamon syrup

Add 8 crushed green cardamom pods to the water, glucose and sugar and bring to the boil. Cool and strain when cold. Perfect with Tangy Lime and Lavender Tart (page 66) and ice cream.

saffron syrup

Add 2–3 pinches of good-quality saffron strands to the finished, hot syrup, and leave to cool. Keep the stamens in the syrup. Good with blancmange, egg custard tart and chilled, creamed rice.

coffee bean syrup

Add 10 fresh coffee beans to the water, glucose and sugar, bring to the boil and leave to cool. Serve with Bitter Chocolate Tart (page 84) and clotted cream, or Bitter Chocolate Mousse (page 89). The coffee beans make a nice garnish for the dessert you serve this with.

rhubarb syrup

Add 225 g (8 oz) of very finely chopped Yorkshire new-season rhubarb to the basic water, glucose and sugar solution. Bring to the boil, cover and leave to cool. This syrup can be strained, or left whole and then folded into chilled, creamed rice, custard or Marzipan Charlotte (page 114).

rosemary flower syrup

150 g (5½ oz) granulated sugar
40 g (1½ oz) light brown soft sugar
about 25 rosemary flower heads

Rosemary flowers are normally in full bloom by the end of March for about two weeks and make the most delicate syrup.

The golden rule when using all flowers in cooking is to make sure you pick them on a sunny day, when the pollen is dry and most fragrant; otherwise the syrup will taste dull.

Place 350 ml (12 fl oz) of cold water and the two sugars in a pan and bring just to the boil. Place the flower heads in a heatproof, screw-top jar and pour on the syrup. Seal the jar and leave in a cool place for about a week.

lemon balm and bay syrup

225 g (8 oz) granulated sugar
10 × 10 cm (4-inch) sprigs of fresh lemon
balm, picked on a bright sunny day
3 small bay leaves, bruised
juice of ½ fresh lime

Pictured opposite is Poached Peaches with Lemon Balm and Bay Syrup (see page 152).

To make the syrup, place the sugar and 275 ml (9½ fl oz) of cold water together in a saucepan and dissolve over a low heat. Put the lemon balm and bay in a sealable jar and pour on the hot syrup, stir in the lime juice and seal. Leave for a minimum of two days or up to one month in a cool place.

rose-petal syrup

4–5 fragrant pink rose heads,
calyxes removed
200 g (7 oz) castor sugar
30 ml (2 tablespoons) liquid glucose
juice of ½ lemon

makes
275 ml (9½ fl oz)

This delicate syrup is still my favourite. Over the past few years the use of roses, or the fragrance of roses, has become very trendy, mostly due to the fact that North-African-, Turkish- and Moroccan-influenced food is being cooked by a lot of restaurants.

For me, the perfume of English roses captured in a light syrup is so magical that you only need a very small amount to get a really rounded flavour. Like all foods in vogue, its misuse is common, a perfect example of not understanding an ingredient before cooking with it. The secret is exactly the same as for picking elderflowers: pick the roses on a warm, sunny day, preferably after lunch to let the dew clear, and make them into syrup straight away.

Rose-petal syrup is perfect with Almond Blancmange (page 21), stirred through rice pudding at the last moment or even poured over ice cream.

Place the rose petals in a sealable, heatproof jar. Bring 225 ml (8 fl oz) of cold water, with the sugar and glucose, to the boil in a pan. Remove from the heat straight away. Pour over the rose petals and seal the jar immediately. Leave until cool.

When cool, add enough lemon juice to bring out the rose flavour. Strain into a clean jar, seal again and leave for a couple of days before using. Keep refrigerated; it will be usable for a couple of weeks.

crème pâtissière

425 ml (14 fl oz) whole milk
1 vanilla pod, split
2 egg yolks
60 g (2 oz) castor sugar
40 g (1½ oz) plain flour, sifted

serves 6–8

Place the milk and vanilla pod in a saucepan and bring to the boil, stirring all the time. Remove from the stove and leave to infuse for 10 minutes.

Meanwhile, whisk the egg yolks and sugar together, until thick and creamy. Add the flour and mix well.

Strain the milk through a fine sieve.

Pour the milk into the egg-yolk mixture, add the vanilla pod then stir well, return to the pan and bring to the boil very slowly, stirring all the time in a figure of eight so no cream catches, until the mixture thickens.

When boiling remove from the heat, and pour into a clean bowl, cover with cling film and leave to cool. Once cool, remove the vanilla pod.

champagne sabayon

6 egg yolks

90 g (3¼ oz) castor sugar

100 ml (3½ fl oz) Champagne or dry
sparkling white wine

finely grated zest of 1 large lime

serves 4

Froths (sabayons) are all the rage at the moment, whether savoury or sweet. They are not new, I was making sweet froths back in the eighties. This version is perfect for summer berries and warm poached peaches. Just take care to whisk all the time once over the simmering water, or you may end up with sweet scrambled egg.

Place the egg yolks, sugar and wine in a heatproof bowl and sit it over a pan of gently simmering water. Whisk until thick, foamy and cooked – to test, lift up a whiskful of sabayon and hold it up against something dark in the kitchen; there should be steam rising from the whisk. This is a good indication of a cooked sabayon. Remove from the heat and add the lime zest.

Spoon over fresh fruit. This sabayon will glaze nicely under a hot grill or a blowtorch, with a sprinkling of icing sugar.

cider sabayon

100 ml (3½ fl oz) dry cider

6 egg yolks

100 g (3½ oz) castor sugar

grated zest and juice of 1 lime

30 ml (2 tablespoons) double cream

serves 4

This froth is perfect with a hearty sweet such as Bramley Apple Puddings (page 32). It's also very nice spooned over poached pears or rhubarb. If cooked and cooled correctly, the sabayon will keep in the fridge for a couple of days.

The sabayon will glaze well under a hot grill or a blowtorch.

Whisk the cider, egg yolks and sugar together over a pan of boiling water until thick and cooked. Continue whisking until completely cold.

Add the lime zest, a touch of lime juice and the cream and whisk in well.

beaumes de venise
sabayon

2 large egg yolks

25 g (1 oz) castor sugar

75 ml (2½ fl oz) Beaumes de Venise

serves 4

Pictured opposite is Iced Charentais Melon with Beaumes de Venise Sabayon, (page 217) and My Mum's Shortbread (page 298).

Place the egg yolks, sugar and wine in a heatproof bowl. Place the bowl over a pan of gently simmering water and immediately start to whisk. Whisk until the foam will hold its own weight, which will take about 4–5 minutes if the egg yolks are at room temperature but a little longer if the yolks are straight from the fridge. The secret with any sabayon is to cook the eggs fairly quickly so you get as much volume into the yolks as possible before they cook completely and hold their own weight.

cherry brandy
crème anglaise

300 ml (½ pint) whole milk

1 vanilla pod, split

6 egg yolks

2 pinches of cornflour or arrowroot

70 g (2½ oz) castor sugar

45–60 ml (3–4 tablespoons) cherry brandy

makes

about 400 ml (14 fl oz)

Very similar to basic Crème Anglaise (opposite), I just add a generous slug of cherry brandy and a touch more cornflour or arrowroot to compensate for the addition of the alcohol. Serve warm with puddings, pies and crumbles and cool with poached fruits and flans.

Place the milk in a pan. Scrape the seeds from the vanilla pod into the milk and then add the pod as well and bring to the boil.

Meanwhile, whisk together the egg yolks, cornflour or arrowroot and castor sugar until thick and pale.

Pour the boiling milk on to the egg-yolk mixture, whisk well and then return to the pan and cook over a very low heat, stirring all the time, until thickened and able to coat the back of the spoon or spatula. Strain through a fine sieve, pushing through all the seeds from the vanilla pod. Finally, stir in the brandy (it's up to you how much you add). Keep warm and covered.

crème anglaise

300 ml (½ pint) whole milk
1 vanilla pod, split
6 egg yolks
70 g (2½ oz) castor sugar
a pinch of cornflour
makes
about 400 ml (14 fl oz)

No pudding book could be complete without a recipe for crème anglaise, a simple and tasty accompaniment to every kind of sweet. Though purists frown on the addition of cornflour, I think it is worth doing as cornflour helps to stabilise the sauce and make it smoother.

Serve this warm with puddings, pies and crumbles or cool with poached fruits or flans.

Place the milk in a saucepan, scrape in the vanilla seeds, add the pod and bring to the boil.

Meanwhile, whisk the egg yolks, sugar and cornflour together until thick and pale. Pour on the boiling milk, whisk well and return to the pan. Cook over a very low heat until the sauce has thickened and is coating the back of the spoon.

Immediately remove from the heat and strain through a sieve, pushing all the vanilla seeds through as well.

fresh coffee sauce

500 ml (18 fl oz) whole milk
75 g (2¾ oz) freshly ground coffee
5 large egg yolks
100 g (3½ oz) castor sugar

makes

about 600 ml (1 pint)

A good sauce not only for mousses but also ice creams, and great with chocolate cake.

Heat the milk and coffee together and bring to the boil, then remove from the heat and allow to infuse for 10 minutes.

Whisk the egg yolks and sugar together until very thick and foamy – the whiter and thicker the eggs and sugar are at this stage, the thicker the sauce will be at the end.

Pour the hot-milk mixture on to the egg yolks and sugar, whisk well, and then return to the pan. Cook over a low heat, stirring continuously, until the mixture thickens and becomes glossy.

Strain the sauce through a fine sieve and then allow to cool. Chill before serving.

bitter chocolate sauce

175 g (6 oz) good-quality cocoa powder
600 ml (1 pint) double cream
40 g (1½ oz) cold unsalted butter, cubed
175 g (6 oz) caster sugar

serves 4

If you like a dark, extra-bitter chocolate sauce, this is the one for you. It makes a great change from the sweet, sickly sauces you can buy and it is easy to make and will keep for two weeks in the fridge, in a sealed container.

You can reheat this in the microwave if necessary.

Place the cocoa powder and cream in a saucepan and bring to the boil. Allow to bubble for 1 minute.

Whisk in the butter, bring back to the boil and cook for a further 1–2 minutes. Strain into a jug or container and cover tightly.

caramelised apricot sauce

250 g (9 oz) castor sugar

420 g can of apricots in syrup, drained

makes

about 450 ml (16 fl oz)

Place the sugar in a pan, add 150 ml (¼ pint) of cold water and then bring to the boil. Cook until it becomes a dark caramel colour. Pour in another 150 ml (¼ pint) of cold water and stand back: the mixture will splutter and splash. Let the syrup come back to the boil and then remove from the heat and swirl the pan around to dissolve the caramel. Allow to cool.

Liquidise the drained apricots and then add cooled caramel syrup until you end up with a nice caramel-flavoured sauce. Cool completely. This sauce is very good with ice cream.

brandy sauce

600 ml (1 pint) whole milk

25 g (1 oz) cornflour, slaked with 60 ml (4 tablespoons) cold water

55 g (2 oz) unrefined granulated sugar

55 g (2 oz) unsalted butter, cut in small cubes

brandy, to taste

makes

about 600 ml (1 pint)

A very simple sauce but nevertheless very good with Christmas pudding. I like to serve double cream as well; why not, after all it's Christmas!

Bring the milk to the boil and then stir in the slaked cornflour. Bring back to the boil, stirring, to thicken.

Remove from the heat and stir in the sugar and butter, until dissolved. Finally, stir in brandy to taste.

Cover and keep warm (I keep mine in a Thermos flask).

raspberry sauce

225 g (8 oz) fresh or good-quality
frozen raspberries
about 100 g (3½ oz) caster sugar
15 ml (1 tablespoon) lemon juice

makes
300 ml (½ pint)

Surprisingly, frozen raspberries are sometimes better than fresh ones for making a sauce; the freezing process seems to draw out the juices better, making a thicker sauce.

Put the raspberries in a liquidiser along with the sugar and lemon juice. Blitz until smooth; you may need to add a touch of cold water to let the sauce down, if it's too thick.

Pass through a fine sieve and check the sweetness; add more sugar or even a touch more lemon to get the right balance.

Chill well before serving.

lime water icing

juice of 1 lime

60–75 ml (4–5 tablespoons) icing sugar

This can also be made with lemon or orange juice but lime has the most powerful flavour.

Sift the icing sugar into a small bowl. Put the lime juice in another small bowl. Gradually mix the icing sugar into the lime juice to make a thin icing.

cream cheese frosting

300 g (10½ oz) cream cheese, softened

70 g (2½ oz) icing sugar, sifted

finely grated zest of 1 orange and juice of

about half an orange

Beat the cream cheese and sugar together until soft. Add the orange zest and then gradually add enough of the orange juice to give a soft consistency. That's it!

cream cheese
and meringue frosting

1 quantity basic meringue (page 131) or a
245 g sachet of Supercook Whisk and
Bake Meringue Mix
25 g (1 oz) castor sugar
150 g (51/2 oz) cream cheese,
whisked until soft
2.5 ml (½ teaspoon) ground mixed spice

makes enough to
cover a 24 cm (9½-inch) diameter cake

This idea just seemed to come out of the blue: it's an alternative to butter-cream icing, which is a thing you either love or hate. With that in mind, I thought it would be nice to create a slightly different icing that would have wider appeal. Everybody seems to like meringue in one way, shape or form – that was the reason I dedicated a whole chapter to this delicious confection – coupling this with the 'afternoon tea' cake idea, this was the result.

I make no bones about the fact I use a sachet of meringue mix, all the reasons for this explained on page 131.

Whisk the meringue until very stiff and then add the castor sugar and whisk again until firm, glossy but still smooth and silky.

Whisk the cream cheese and mixed spice together in a separate bowl. Slowly and gently beat the meringue and cream cheese mixtures together.

Spread on to the cake, covering it completely so you end up with a fluffy-looking cake. Chill for 1 hour or longer (overnight if possible) before eating; this will firm up the meringue and set the cream cheese perfectly.

royal icing

1.5 kg (3 lb 5 oz) icing sugar, sifted

40 g (1½ oz) 'Meri White' (powdered egg white)

about 15 ml (1 tablespoon) glycerine (available from chemists)

makes enough

to coat a 30 cm (12-inch) cake twice

Make sure the icing sugar is sifted at least twice just to be on the safe side.

Place the dry egg white powder in a clean mixing bowl, add 275 ml (9½ fl oz) of cold water and stir with a fork until frothy. Pour into the bowl of a food mixer or use a hand-held whisk.

Add half of the icing sugar to the egg mixture. Set the machine to a medium speed and beat slowly until you have a smooth paste – if you beat it too fast you will end up with lots of air bubbles in the finished icing and, once it has dried, there will be tiny holes, so be patient. Add the rest of the icing sugar and beat to a firm paste. The icing should fall off a spoon when tapped slightly. Add a little extra water if too thick or a little more icing sugar if the icing is too thin.

Finally, add the glycerine and mix carefully and well. Keep covered with cling film until needed, up to 2 hours.

For instructions on how to cover a cake with marzipan and royal icing, see page 255.

real butter cream

280 g (10 oz) unrefined icing sugar, sifted
6 large egg yolks
450 g (1 lb) softened but not runny unsalted
butter, cut into small cubes
squeeze of lemon juice,

makes enough

to cover a 23 cm (9-inch) diameter × 3 cm
(1½-inch) deep Victoria sponge

As children, we always had butter-cream-filled cakes. Sadly, these days butter cream has fallen from grace, basically due to our obsession with healthy eating. Most butter-cream recipes just use butter or even margarine beaten with sugar to form a sweet greasy stodge but adding egg yolks makes the icing light and very creamy.

This recipe was used by the Queen's pastry chef, an old college lecturer of mine by the name of Brian Gilham, probably the best 'old-school' pastry chef I have ever met. His attention to detail was second to none, I owe this man a great deal.

This recipe is light and not greasy at all, a real treat.

Whisk together the sugar, egg yolks and 150 ml (¼ pint) of cold water in a heatproof bowl over a pan of gently simmering water until thick, foamy and cooked – this will take about 10 minutes. I find it's best to use an electric hand-whisk.

Remove the bowl from the heat and whisk at high speed until cool and very thick (you can transfer it to a food mixer at this point, if you like).

Whisk in the soft butter a little at a time so you end up with a light, creamy icing. Finally add the lemon juice.

Remove from the bowl and pipe or spread over cakes, or use to fill Japonaises (page 135) or Brandy Snaps (page 291).

coffee butter cream
Add 30 ml (2 tablespoons) of strong coffee to the egg yolks.

vanilla butter cream
Add a few drops of vanilla extract to the yolks.

hazelnut butter cream
Add 115 g (4 oz) chopped browned hazelnuts.

CAKES

When we were growing up, my mother cooked a huge number of cakes and biscuits. Our first real taste of other cakes started when Grandma Vickery used to buy us what we termed 'shop cakes' every Tuesday. Suddenly we had wonderful cakes, such as cream horns with their crunchy, sugary tops, large Viennese whirls with their buttery, crumbly texture, chocolate swiss rolls and giant fresh cream meringues. The only trouble was that there were three of us – all boys – and we could never agree on who got what. There was always a boring macaroon that we kids hated; it had no cream, no visible sugar and it was smaller than everything else. Dad would make us draw lots to stop the bickering. Even then we would whinge and fight afterwards.

In spite of all this I was inspired to look out for cakes. I loved bakery windows crammed full of beautifully finished and decorated pastries, wedding cakes and buns. The fantastically clever way bakers go about their business still really amazes me.

There was a time when I was at college when I really wanted to become a professional confectioner. I bought French cookery books and marvelled at their pâtisserie photos. What really did it for me was the photograph of a strawberry gâteau in the book, *Great Chefs of France* by Anthony Blake and Quentin Crewe. The cake is beautiful to look at, with perfect colouring, decoration and filigree, and the way the halved strawberries are set in the side of the cake blew me away. This spurred me on to getting an unpaid job in a bakery on my day off to learn the trade. The chap was very nice and said I could have a lie-in and start at 4 am (he started at 1 am!). It was invaluable experience and I really enjoyed the time with him. In my next job I met a French pastry chef called Jean

who was close to retiring. One day we got chatting over staff lunch and I asked him about France and the pastry shops. He told me he used to work in a pâtisserie and said if I wanted him to show me, I had to come in at 5 in the morning. So I did exactly that for the following year. He taught me so much and I can never thank him enough. It was a great start for a 19 year old.

My love of cakes and bakery has never waned. Recently I made a small film in Pâtisserie Valerie in Soho and I realised that, after 20 years in the trade, I still got a buzz from watching Robert, the larger-than-life owner, and his head baker producing wonderful wedding and celebration cakes. They produce an average of 15 wedding cakes on a Saturday, all hand-finished, delivered and perfect. Thank goodness this unique art is still alive and well.

rich christmas
fruit cake

500 g (1 lb 2 oz) unsalted butter, softened

500 g (1 lb 2 oz) soft brown sugar

8 eggs

500 g (1 lb 2 oz) plain white flour

450 g (1 lb) currants

450 g (1 lb) fat sultanas

450 g (1 lb) raisins or chopped dates

225 g (8 oz) whole natural coloured glacé cherries

175 g (6 oz) chopped mixed candied peel

10 ml (2 teaspoons) ground mixed spice

10 ml (2 teaspoons) ground allspice

10 ml (2 teaspoons) vanilla powder

85 g (3 oz) ground almonds

85 g (3 oz) slivered almonds

20 ml (4 teaspoons) black treacle

60 ml (4 tablespoons) malt whisky

30 ml (2 tablespoons) heather or other clear honey

finely grated zest and juice of 1 large lemon

finely grated zest of 1 large orange and juice of ½ the orange

to decorate

1.25 kg (2 lb 12 oz) natural-coloured marzipan

royal icing (page 250)

makes

a 28 cm (11-inch) cake

serves 10–12

This classic cake is based on my mum's recipe, all I have done is added honey, whisky and mixed peel (she detests the stuff).

Christmas or rich fruit cakes like these are relatively easy to make. The two main problems are the shopping and the cooking. I spend hours walking around the supermarket trying to get all the bits and pieces together and the cooking needs to be taken slowly: this cake needs at least 5½ hours. It can be made up to three months in advance.

Preheat the oven to 140°C/275°F/Gas Mark 1. Line a 28 cm (11-inch) round cake tin with at least two layers of greaseproof or silicone paper, leaving at least 4 cm (1¾ inches) sticking up above the sides of the tin. Wrap two layers of brown paper around the outside of the tin and tie with heatproof string to secure.

Soften the butter but do not let it melt, then add the sugar and beat well until very light, pale and creamy. Whisk the eggs together and gradually add to the butter mixture in small amounts, taking care to beat well after every small amount of egg. Take care towards the end as the mixture will separate very easily; if it does curdle, add 55 g (2 oz) of the flour before continuing to add the rest of the egg.

When the egg has been fully incorporated, fold in the flour, dried fruits and all the rest of the dry ingredients carefully; do not overwork. Finally, stir in the treacle, whisky, honey and fruit zests and juices, and that's it.

Carefully spoon into the tin, cover loosely with greaseproof paper and bake for about 5½ hours, removing the greaseproof paper from the top after about 4½ hours.

To test whether the cake is cooked, insert a metal skewer or the blade of a small, sharp knife in the centre; it should be clean when removed with no mixture sticking to it. When cooked, remove from the oven and leave to cool for 30 minutes before turning out on to a cooling rack. Leave to cool overnight.

Decorate to your own design then add ribbons and bits and pieces once dried. Cover with marzipan, at least 2 cm (¾ inch) thick and ice with royal icing, giving it at least three coats (see instructions below), or of course ready-made, ready-to-roll icing. You can, of course, decorate with glazed candied fruits and a thick ribbon, for a different Christmas look.

how to cover a cake with marzipan and royal icing

Remove any paper from the cake and place on a chopping board. With a sharp serrated knife, carefully cut the top of the cake off evenly, so you have a perfectly crisp edge. It looks like you are wasting a lot of cake but this makes the end-product much easier to marzipan and ice and also looks a lot neater.

Heat 90 ml (6 tablespoons) of apricot jam with 45 ml (3 tablespoons) of cold water and stir together until smooth.

Unwrap all the marzipan blocks and knead well together until soft and supple; you may need to use a little cornflour to stop the marzipan sticking. Cut off about one-third of the marzipan and roll into a ball. Then flatten to roughly the diameter of the cake, trying to keep the marzipan as thick as possible.

Brush what will be the top of the cake (actually the bottom) with apricot jam and then invert the cake on to the marzipan and press down well. The marzipan should fit well; trim off any excess.

Add the excess to the rest of the marzipan and knead well. Leave the cake inverted so it sits on top of the marzipan.

Cut a piece of string long enough to go around the circumference of the cake and allow an extra 4 cm (1¾ inches) roughly. Roll the marzipan out to a long sausage roughly the length of the string, and then carefully, using a rolling pin, roll the sausage flat and as evenly as possible to the depth of the cake, plus the marzipan already on the top of the cake. I find it's easier to use another piece of string as a guide. Trim the marzipan with a sharp knife on both sides so it's the exact width of the cake.

Lightly brush the side of the cake with apricot jam and then carefully roll up the marzipan like a large swiss roll.

Place the end of the marzipan on the side of the cake so it's flush with the board or work surface, and stick well, then very carefully unwrap the roll around the cake, taking care to press it evenly, until you reach the point you started from. Finally roll over the top of the other marzipan from where you started, then cut straight through both pieces and remove the excess, gently push together, you should have a perfect seal.

Turn the cake over and seal the top edge of marzipan, you should now have a totally even and covered cake. Re-roll the top and sides with a rolling pin to really smooth out the marzipan. Then 'polish', basically, rubbing your hand all over the marzipan quickly; this warms the oils in the marzipan and brings out a nice shine and smoothness.

Place 15 ml (1 tablespoon) of royal icing on a silver cake board and smooth out slightly. Place the cake on the board and press down, check that it's central and leave to dry, preferably overnight in an airing cupboard or warm kitchen. This part is quite important if you plan to keep the cake for any length of time, as the drying process stops the oils from the almonds spoiling the royal icing on the cake. Some bakers brush the marzipan with lightly beaten egg white to seal and dry, but that's up to you.

I find the best way to ice a cake is to do it in four stages. Firstly, spoon a thick layer of icing around the outside of the cake trying to make it as even as possible. Then, with a palette knife, even out further still.

Using a large stainless-steel scraper and a turntable, place the scraper at exactly 90° to the cake, carefully turn the turntable and a smooth edge will start to appear, carry on until you end up at the point you started, then pull the scraper away at an angle. Don't worry too much at this point about getting it perfect, just aim to get it even and fairly smooth. With a wet cloth, wipe any icing off the board. Trim all the icing from the top of the cake with a palette knife and leave to dry for at least 36 hours.

Once it's dried, you can ice the top. Spoon over the icing the same thickness as before and even out with a stainless-steel ruler or palette knife. Gently spin the cake around on the turntable and gently paddle the icing, by this I mean make small indentations keeping the palette knife flat to the cake to remove any air bubbles.

Take a stainless-steel ruler or long, sturdy knife and, starting at one side of the cake, as evenly as possible draw the rule across the cake towards you, so you end up with a completely smooth top to the cake. Again, do not worry too much about getting the top too smooth, this will get easier as you add more coats. Trim the edges and leave to dry again for 36 hours.

Once dried lightly sand with sand paper and shave with a sharp knife to remove any bumps and spare icing.

Repeat both processes again so you end up with a very smooth finished cake. I sometimes do this three or four times to get it right. It does take a bit of practice but is well worth it.

You can of course use the ready-rolled icing, I do rather think it's cheating but, having said that, I admit that it's much, much quicker to use ready-rolled, which is a very good product and extremely versatile.

twelfth-night cake

500 g (1 lb 2 oz) puff pastry (page 42)
125 g (4½ oz) unsalted butter
125 g (4½ oz) castor sugar
1 large egg, plus 1 large egg yolk,
lightly beaten
40 g (1½ oz) plain white flour, sifted
125 g (4½ oz) ground almonds
30 ml (2 tablespoons) brandy
finely grated zest of 1 orange and 1 lemon
45 ml (3 tablespoons) apricot jam
king charm and dried bean
beaten egg, for glazing
icing sugar, to decorate

serves 8

This version is based on a recipe sent to me from my good friend and colleague Mary Cadogan, a very clever and informative writer. She got the original from a French nanny who used to work for her. Like many good food ideas that were invented in Britain, however, the French seemed to have hijacked it from the Victorians originally. I have a suspicion that the history of this lovely cake goes even further back: it was traditionally eaten at Epiphany (6th January). Anyway, it's good fun and very tasty indeed.

The tradition is to hide a gold king charm and a dried pea or bean in the sponge. When the cake is cut, the person who gets the charm is king for the day, and will have good luck for the rest of the year. The person who gets the bean or pea gets to do all the washing-up or, if adults are playing, gets to buy the next bottle of bubbly. No doubt we will soon have some sort of Brussels directive, saying that there is a danger of choking if the king is swallowed and dishing out huge fines and jail sentences to people who dare cook this cake! So, I suggest you cook it while you still can.

Cut the puff pastry in half, and roll out both pieces nice and thinly, to make two circles about 23 cm (9 inches) in diameter. Place one piece of pastry on a greased baking tray and then the other on a plate, chill both for about 20 minutes.

Preheat the oven to 200°C/400°F/Gas Mark 6. Beat the butter and sugar together until thick and white and then add the beaten egg a little at a time. Carefully fold in the flour and ground almonds; finally, add the brandy and zests.

Mark an 18 cm (7-inch) diameter circle on the puff pastry on the baking sheet. Spread the apricot jam on the chilled pastry, keeping it inside the marked circle.

Pipe or spoon the almond mixture on top of the jam in a slight mound, again keeping within the inner circle. Press the king charm and bean into the mixture, keeping them apart. Brush beaten egg over the edge of the pastry, lay the other piece of pastry on top and press the edges together firmly.

Cut out a scalloped edge. Using the back of a knife, draw in the sides at frequent intervals so the edge is neat and well sealed. Brush beaten egg all over.

Using the back of a knife, mark a crown design in the middle of the pastry for decoration, but only cut about halfway through the pastry, don't go all the way. Make a small incision in the top to allow steam to escape and then bake for about 40 minutes, or until well risen and golden (the oven must be hot for this to work, or the pastry will fall away)

Remove the cooked cake from the oven, dust lightly with icing sugar and return to the oven for a further 15 minutes or so, until golden brown and glazed – take care as the cake can catch and burn.

Cool, then serve in large slices, remembering to let your guests know about the hard bits. In Victorian England, the cake would have been served with brandy butter and/or cream.

carrot cake

with cream cheese and orange frosting

85 g (3 oz) madeira cake crumbs
55 g (2 oz) plain white flour, sifted
15 g (½ oz) baking powder
250 g (9 oz) skinned hazelnuts, chopped
300 g (10½ oz) grated and well
squeezed out carrot
15 ml (1 tablespoon) rum
5 large eggs, separated
240 g (8½ oz) castor sugar
2 large pinches of ground cinnamon
grated zest of 1 large lemon
5 ml (1 teaspoon) vanilla extract or powder
60 ml (4 tablespoons) apricot jam
500 g (1 lb 2 oz) natural-colour marzipan
1 quantity Caramelised Apricot Sauce
(page 244)

for the frosting
400 g (14 oz) cream cheese
finely grated zest of 1 orange, plus the
juice from ½ the orange
85 g (3 oz) icing sugar, sifted
makes
a 25 cm (10-inch) cake

I love this cake, it's so moist and delicate. I normally coat mine in tempered bitter chocolate, but here I'm using cream-cheese icing, a twist on passion cake. Be careful to squeeze any juice out of the carrots very well, and then weigh them after that.

The only thing to serve with this is Caramelised Apricot Sauce, a great foil to the rich sponge.

Preheat the oven to 190°C/375°F/Gas Mark 5. Grease and line a 25 cm (10-inch) diameter × 6 cm (5½-inch) deep, loose-bottomed cake tin.

Mix the madeira crumbs with the flour and baking powder. Add the hazelnuts and carrot and mix well. Next, whisk the rum, egg yolks and 125 g (4½ oz) of castor sugar together until thick and foamy. Fold in the cinnamon, zest and vanilla.

Whisk the egg whites until they are thick and foamy, add the remaining 115 g (4 oz) of castor sugar and whisk until firm and glossy. Fold the madeira crumb mixture into the egg yolks, then finally add the meringue. Spoon into the tin and bake for 30 minutes.

Check to see if the cake has set, using a skewer or small, sharp knife. You should be able to withdraw it without any uncooked mixture clinging to it. If so, reduce the heat to 160°C/325°F/Gas Mark 3, and cook for about a further 15 minutes or until nicely browned and firm to the touch. If not, cook for a few minutes more and test again before reducing the oven temperature. Allow to cool.

Remove the cake from the tin. Warm and sieve the apricot jam. Spread the top and sides of the cake all over with jam. Roll out the marzipan as thinly as possible so it is about 6 cm (5½ inches) bigger than the cake all around and then place centrally on top of the cake. Press on to the sides and top and leave to dry slightly.

To make the cream-cheese frosting, beat the cream cheese with the icing sugar and orange zest, adding the juice to loosen the mixture slightly. Spread frosting evenly on to the cake. Cut and serve with the apricot sauce.

simnel cake

500 g (1 lb 2 oz) natural-colour marzipan

225 g (8 oz) unsalted butter, softened

225 g (8 oz) unrefined castor sugar

4 eggs, beaten

225 g (8 oz) self-raising white flour

25 g (1 oz) ground almonds

2.5 ml (½ teaspoon) ground allspice

2.5 ml (½ teaspoon) ground mace

2.5 ml (½ teaspoon) ground cinnamon

2.5 ml (½ teaspoon) freshly grated nutmeg

225 g (8 oz) currants

115 g (4 oz) sultanas

100 g (3½ oz) glacé cherries, washed and chopped

55 g (2 oz) candied peel, chopped very finely

finely grated zest of 2 lemons

30 ml (2 tablespoons) brandy

30 ml (2 tablespoons) apricot jam, to glaze

1 small egg, beaten, to glaze

for the icing

about 60 ml (4 tablespoons) golden icing sugar, sifted

juice of 1 lime, strained

makes

a 20 cm (8-inch) cake

This traditional cake has many stories attached to it, ranging from the tale that it was a cake made by young girls in service to take home on leave at Easter, to that of a couple who could not agree on whether to cook a fruit cake or sponge for Easter. They were supposedly called Simon and Nellie, so they called the cake 'Sim-Nel'.

The decoration is very traditional, layered with marzipan, grilled with twelve balls of marzipan on top, each one representing one of the apostles. Some people say that one should be removed, to represent Judas, others say an extra one should be added to represent Jesus. It's really up to you. This cake is very Lancastrian, especially popular around Bury.

You'll also need a wide ribbon and a posh box to put this beautiful cake in!

Preheat the oven to 160°C/325°F/Gas Mark 3. Butter a deep 20 cm (8-inch) diameter cake tin and line with a double layer of greaseproof paper. Cut an 85 g (3 oz) piece off the marzipan and reserve, then cut the remaining marzipan in half.

Cream the soft butter and sugar together until thick and creamy. Beat in the eggs one at a time, then fold in the flour, almonds and spices. Finally, stir in the dried fruit, cherries, peel, lemon zest and brandy. Use half the mixture to fill the bottom of the prepared tin.

Roll out one of the larger pieces of marzipan into a circle just large enough to fit into the cake tin. Lay carefully over the cake mixture, pressing down to expel any air bubbles. Spoon in the rest of the cake mixture and level out. Bake for about 1 hour 40–1 hour 50 minutes, or until set and nicely browned. Test with a skewer in the normal way; if the skewer comes out clean, the cake is cooked. Remove from the oven and allow to cool.

Warm and sieve the apricot jam. Take the cooled cake out of the tin and remove the paper, then trim the top flat if necessary and turn the cake upside-down. Brush a little jam over what is now the top. Roll out the remaining larger piece of marzipan to fit the top of the cake perfectly, press down on top with your hands and roll flat with a rolling pin. Decorate the edge of the marzipan using a 'pinching' effect. Divide the reserved 85 g (3 oz) marzipan into eleven, twelve or thirteen balls. Brush a little beaten egg on the marzipan on top of the cake and stick down the balls along the edge.

Place the cake on a baking sheet and brown under a hot grill.

Gradually mix enough icing sugar into the lime juice to give a runny consistency. Pour into the middle of the cake and allow to set. Wrap a large ribbon around the side of the cake so you can just see the cake and marzipan.

fresh strawberry
mille-feuille

about 200 g (7 oz) puff pastry (page 42)
or a 28 × 23 cm (11- × 9-inch) sheet
of frozen puff pastry

10 ml (2 teaspoons) vanilla extract
30 ml (2 tablespoons) icing sugar,
plus extra for dusting
300 ml (½ pint) double cream,
lightly whipped
60 ml (4 tablespoons) strawberry preserve
or good-quality jam
300 g (10½ oz) fresh English strawberries,
hulled and halved
flaked almonds, toasted, to decorate
(optional)

serves 4–6

The best things about the English summer, I believe, are strawberries and raspberries. Having been a pastry chef for more years than I can remember, there is nothing I like better than making these wonderful berries into all sorts of glorious sweets, tarts and puddings. Most of the strawberries and raspberries grown commercially these days are devoid of real colour and flavour and are frankly not worth the effort but, if you are lucky enough to pick your own or, better still, grow your own, I can assure you that you'll never touch a tasteless impostor again.

Over the years I have been very lucky to have found and worked with a number of people who have been passionate about growing or rearing different varieties of foods for me. One who stands out is Mr Sage, who grew the most fantastic soft fruit, ranging from the largest and tastiest blackberries you have ever set your eyes on to the most perfumed strawberries and sweetest raspberries you will ever find. Two varieties to keep a look out for are 'Mara de Bois' strawberries and 'Autumn Bliss' raspberries, to me they are the best and cannot be beaten. The recipe here is the only way to eat strawberries, apart from just with cream.

Preheat the oven to 200°C/400°F/Gas Mark 6. Unwrap the puff pastry carefully, place on a non-stick baking sheet and prick really well with a fork. Bake for about 15–20 minutes or until nicely risen and golden brown. Take care with puff pastry because it tends to burn very quickly once you take your eye off it. Once cooked, remove from the oven and transfer to a cooling rack to allow to cool.

Next, add the vanilla and icing sugar to the cream and stir together, do not over beat or the cream will separate. Keep as cold as possible.

Cut the pastry into three equal pieces. Spread the strawberry jam over two of the layers (this is a novel idea but not only does it sweeten the dessert but it also brings out the flavour of the strawberries). Place the halved strawberries on top of the strawberry jam. Using a palette knife spread a thick layer of the cream mixture on top of the strawberries and jam.

Use the palette knife carefully to lift one of the covered pieces of pastry on top of the other and nestle it down nicely. Top with the final piece of puff

baby coffee éclairs

1 quantity choux pastry (page 44)

1 egg, beaten

for the coffee pastry cream

300 ml (½ pint) whole milk

10 g (¼ oz) freshly ground coffee

4 large egg yolks

60 g (2¼ oz) unrefined castor sugar

60 g (2¼ oz) plain white flour, sifted

300 ml (½ pint) double cream,
lightly whipped

for the icing

25 ml (5 teaspoons) instant coffee

45 ml (3 tablespoons) boiling water

about 250 g (9 oz) Tate and Lyle
Fondant Icing Sugar

makes

60–70 baby éclairs

Preheat the oven to 220°C/425°F/Gas Mark 7. Very lightly grease two baking sheets. Spoon the choux pastry into a large piping bag fitted with a 1.5 cm (⅝ inch) nozzle. Pipe the pastry on the baking sheets into 4 cm (1¾-inch) long éclairs. Brush with beaten egg and re-shape at the same time. Bake for 15–20 minutes, or until well risen and golden.

Once they are fully formed and golden, turn the oven down to 160°C/325°F/Gas Mark 3 and cook the éclairs for a further 5–10 minutes to dry them out until they are very crisp. This is very important as, the crisper they are, the easier they are to pipe and ice. It also ensures that you do not end up with raw choux pastry inside. Remove from the oven and cool completely – don't store them in an airtight container as this makes the pastry soggy.

Meanwhile, make the pastry cream: bring the milk and ground coffee to the boil in a pan, stirring all the time. Remove from the heat and leave to infuse for 10 minutes.

Meanwhile, whisk the egg yolks and sugar together. Add the flour and mix well. Strain the milk through a fine sieve on to the egg and sugar mixture and stir well. Return to the pan and bring to the boil very slowly, stirring all the time in a figure of eight so it doesn't catch. Once boiling, remove from the heat and pour into a clean bowl. Cover with cling film and leave to cool.

Whisk the cooled coffee pastry cream to loosen and break it down, then add the whipped cream and whisk together. Spoon into a piping bag fitted with a 5 mm (¼-inch) nozzle. Using a small knife, make small incisions in the base of each éclair large enough to fit the nozzle. Pipe the coffee cream into the éclairs one by one, until they feel heavy and full.

Mix together the instant coffee and boiling water, then gradually add enough fondant icing sugar to make an icing of coating consistency. Dip each éclair into the icing one at a time and smooth off with your finger. Leave to set for 15 minutes and then serve piled high.

baby bakewells
with lime water icing

250 g (9 oz) shortbread pastry (page 45)

for the sponge filling
125 g (4½ oz) unsalted butter, softened
125 g (4½ oz) castor sugar
1 large egg, plus 1 large egg yolk, beaten
125 g (4½ oz) ground almonds
40 g (1½ oz) plain white flour, sifted
15 ml (1 tablespoon) crème pâtissière
(optional) (see page 235)
45 ml (3 tablespoons) raspberry jam or jelly
about 30 flaked almonds
Lime Water Icing (page 247), to decorate

makes
about 30 baby bakewells

Most people have eaten bakewell tart at some time in their lives but the trouble with most bakewells is that they are flavoured with almond essence, which, frankly, tastes nothing like real almonds. I would sooner eat the real thing: the taste is completely different. These are great as an afternoon tea or an autumn pudding.

Just use good-quality almonds and make sure to beat the butter and castor sugar for the sponge filling until the mixture is really pale.

Preheat the oven to 220°C/425°F/Gas Mark 7. Grease two mini muffin tins.

Only rolling out half the mixture at a time so the dough does not get too warm, roll out the shortbread dough until the pastry is about 5 mm (¼ inch) thick. Cut out circles with a pastry cutter approximately 2 cm (¾ inch) larger than the diameter of the muffin cups and press the dough carefully into the tins. Repeat until you have lined all the tins and then chill for 30 minutes before use. There is no need to bake the pastry blind as it will cook very quickly; also it's nice to eat these tarts slightly undercooked.

Beat the soft butter and castor sugar together until soft and white. Gradually add the beaten egg until the mixture is thick and creamy.

Fold in the almonds and sifted flour carefully and add the crème pâtissière, if using (this just makes the finished sponge richer). If you're not ready to cook the tartlets, you can chill the mixture at this stage.

Spoon the mixture into a piping bag fitted with a medium nozzle (if the mixture has been chilled pop it into the microwave just to warm it through enough to be able to pipe easily).

Spoon a little raspberry jam into each lined muffin tin and then pipe in the sponge mixture so it comes about three-quarters of the way up. Top each with a flaked almond. Bake in the oven for 12–15 minutes, or until well risen and golden brown. Allow to cool.

Mix together the lime juice and icing sugar to make a thin icing and drizzle over the top of the tarts; then leave to set. Serve with a large blob of clotted cream.

roasted hazelnut
shortcakes

175 g (6 oz) blanched hazelnuts

175 g (6 oz) unsalted butter, not too cold

115 g (4 oz) castor sugar

225 g (8 oz) plain white flour

a pinch of salt

makes

about 18 shortcakes

This is an unusual shortbread but simple to make; the secret is to make sure that the nuts are cold when added to the mixture, or the oil that is released will make the shortbread very difficult to roll out and it won't hold its shape once in the oven (the shortbread is already fairly high in butter).

Sandwich larger discs of this shortbread with fresh ripe, white peaches, and double cream sweetened slightly with icing sugar and vanilla, to make a great summer dessert.

Preheat the oven to 200°C/400°F/Gas Mark 6. Place the hazelnuts on a baking tray and cook in the oven for about 5–8 minutes, shaking occasionally, until the nuts are lightly brown. Remove from the oven and leave to cool completely.

Chop the cooled hazelnuts with a large knife or in a food processor, not too finely or too much oil will be released (but if they are too large it will be difficult to roll the dough out thinly enough!). Aim for pieces the size of coarse breadcrumbs.

Place the butter and sugar in a mixing bowl and beat until soft and blended – it shouldn't be too whipped and creamy. Add the flour, salt and hazelnuts and then mix together to form a soft dough. Roll into a sausage shape (this makes it much easier to roll out when chilled), wrap in cling film and for about 30 minutes.

When chilled, roll the dough out quickly to about 5 mm (¼ inch) thick and use a 7 cm (3-inch) diameter cutter to cut out the biscuits. Place the biscuits on a greased baking tray and cook in the oven for about 8–10 minutes or until just golden brown.

Allow the biscuits to cool on the baking sheet before attempting to move them, as they are very fragile. If you find they have stuck to the tray once cooled, just pop the tray back in the oven for 30 seconds to release them. Store in an airtight container, layered with paper napkins or greaseproof paper, for up to a week.

brandy snaps

225 g (8 oz) castor sugar
2 pinches of ground ginger
125 g (4½ oz) unsalted butter, softened
115 g (4 oz) plain white flour
115 g (4 oz) golden syrup

makes
about 70 brandy snaps

These are nice filled with thick cream flavoured with a little vanilla, or shape them over an upturned small bowl to make decorative baskets in which to serve ice cream or sorbets, especially Pink Champagne Sorbet with Double Cream (page 196). The recipe makes a large quantity but can easily be halved.

Slightly cream together the sugar, ginger and butter. Add the flour and golden syrup and mix to a firm paste. Roll into a long sausage about 3.5 cm (1½ inches) in diameter and then wrap tightly in cling film, making sure not to catch the cling film inside the roll. Chill well (overnight is best).

Preheat the oven to 180°C/350°F/Gas Mark 4. Lightly grease a baking tray.

Remove the cling film from the sausage and cut off 5 mm (¼-inch) thick slices. Arrange the slices on the baking tray, spacing them out well. Bake for about 8–10 minutes, or until well spread out and golden.

Remove from the oven and leave to cool for a few seconds to firm up slightly. Using a spatula or fish slice carefully remove one brandy snap at a time from the baking sheet and then straightaway loosely wrap it around the handle of a wooden spoon to shape into a roll (if the brandy snaps cool too quickly and start to break, a good tip is to replace the baking tray in the oven for a minute or so to soften them up again slightly). Once shaped, leave to cool.

Slide the cooled brandy snaps off the spoon handles and store in an airtight container for three or four days.

almond butter crisp

8 sheets of filo pastry
55 g (2 oz) unsalted butter, melted
about 50 ml (10 teaspoons)
golden icing sugar, sifted
finely grated zest of 1 lemon
100 g (3½ oz) slivered almonds

serves 6

This is similar to the Greek baklava, sweet, sticky and delicious. Once you start eating it, it's difficult to stop and, as well as being a teatime treat, it makes a great pudding.

Preheat the oven to 160°C/325°F/Gas Mark 3. Grease a non-stick baking sheet.

Lay the filo pastry sheets on top of one another on a chopping board and, with a very sharp knife, cut out 20 cm (8-inch) circles, using a plate as a guide. Cover with a slightly damp tea towel.

Place one sheet of pastry on the baking sheet and brush over some of the butter. Sprinkle with about 7.5 ml (1½ teaspoons) of icing sugar and all of the lemon zest and then add a layer of almonds.

Place another layer of pastry on top, brush over more butter, sprinkle with 7.5 ml (1½ teaspoons) of icing sugar and some of the almonds. Repeat this process using another five circles of pastry.

Place the remaining pastry circle on top of the layered cake, brush a little butter over the top and loosely cover with cling film. Chill well for 15 minutes.

Remove the cling film and bake the chilled cake for 15–20 minutes, or until crisp and lightly browned all over.

Cool slightly and cut into six wedges, then allow to cool completely. This will keep for a day, left uncovered.

lavender shortbread

500 g (1 lb 2 oz) shortbread dough

(pate sablé, page 45)

10 fresh lavender heads

makes

10–12 shortbreads

Lavender is a flavour that you either love or hate; there doesn't seem to be any middle ground. I didn't really use it much in cooking until recently, because it reminded me of drawers of winter clothes.

Fern planted several varieties of lavender in the garden but, to be honest, I didn't pay much attention to them until last summer. Then on one hot day I happened to walk past the bushes and, as I brushed against them, the heady perfume that came from the plants was staggering. So, with this in mind, I started to play around with the flavour. I'm still not too sure about using lavender in savoury dishes as it has too perfumed an aroma; still, perhaps that's what some people would say about rosemary?

Cut off the top 5 cm (2 inches) of the lavender heads and discard the stems. Finely chop the lavender tips and flowers. Add the chopped lavender to the flour as you make the pate sablé and chill for 20 minutes.

Preheat the oven to 190°C/375°F/Gas Mark 5. Lightly grease a baking sheet. Roll out the dough to no more than 1 cm (½ inch) thick and then use an 8 cm (3½-inch) cutter to cut out 10–12 discs; the mixture is quite unstable so take care. Transfer to the baking sheet. Bake the shortbreads for 15–20 minutes or until lightly browned.

Take the shortbreads out of the oven and allow to cool for about 10 minutes, to allow the butter to set. Then carefully take them off the baking sheet and transfer to a cooling rack to cool completely. Store in an airtight container for up to a week.

soft custard cookies
with white chocolate

115 g (4 oz) unsalted butter, softened

115 g (4 oz) castor sugar

90 g (3¼ oz) white chocolate, finely chopped

200 g (7 oz) self-raising flour

100 g (3½ oz) cold Bird's custard, made to packet instructions

makes

about 20 cookies

I nicked this idea from a friend of mine in America; all I did was add the custard and chocolate.

The taste of white chocolate really brings out the flavour of the custard – just remember to chop the chocolate finely or the dough will be difficult to cut. The mixture can be frozen and cut off as needed. The cookies will be soft and moist.

Cream the soft butter and sugar until white and creamy. Add the chocolate, flour and custard and mix well.

Form into a sausage shape, roughly 5 cm (2 inches) in diameter, roll in cling film or baking parchment and chill or freeze for about an hour.

Preheat the oven to 180°C/350°F/Gas Mark 4. Make sure the sausage is very cold before you attempt to cut, then cut off 1.5 cm (⅝-inch) thick slices, peel off the cling film or paper and place on a greased baking sheet, spacing them out well as they will spread as they cook. Bake for about 12–15 minutes or until the edges are golden and the tops are a pale creamy colour.

Remove from the oven and allow to cool slightly before trying to lift off the hot tray. Store in an airtight container for up to a week.

glacé cherry
shortbreads

175 g (6 oz) unsalted butter, softened

115 g (4 oz) castor sugar

2 egg yolks

225 g (8 oz) plain white flour

about 100 g (3½ oz) glacé cherries, halved

makes

about 28 small rosettes

A nice, very rich, shortbread biscuit that also makes an easy petit four.

Preheat the oven to 190°C/375°F/Gas Mark 5. Lightly grease two baking trays.

Beat the butter and sugar together until very pale and creamy. Add the egg yolks and mix well, then add the flour and bring together to form a soft mixture – the softer the mixture, the easier it will be to pipe out. Spoon into a large piping bag fitted with a 1 cm (½-inch) fluted nozzle.

Carefully pipe 4 cm (1¾-inch) diameter rosettes on to the baking sheets, spacing them out to allow for spreading. Top each with a cherry half and press down gently. Bake in the oven for about 10 minutes, or until light golden brown. Allow to cool slightly on the baking sheets before transferring to a cooling rack. Store in an airtight container for up to a week.

my mum's shortbread

225 g (8 oz) plain white flour

115 g (4 oz) cornflour

225 g (8 oz) unsalted butter, softened

55 g (2 oz) castor sugar

55 g (2 oz) icing sugar, sifted

a couple of drops of vanilla extract or

a large pinch of vanilla powder

makes

about 20 biscuits

A good shortbread biscuit for eating with tea; my father thinks it's too rich, but I think it's great, Mum! This recipe is good for biscuits but unsuitable for lining tins and moulds, as it is very fragile.

Sift the flour and cornflour together. Beat the butter and sugars together in a bowl until soft and fluffy. Add the vanilla extract or powder to the butter and sugar mixture along with the flour and cornflour then knead well to make a dough. Shape into a ball then flatten and wrap in cling film. Chill for about 30 minutes.

Preheat the oven to 180°C/350°F/Gas Mark 4. Grease two baking sheets.

Roll out the dough to about 5 mm (¼ inch) thick and then use a 7 cm (3-inch) diameter cutter to cut out the biscuits. Place on the baking sheets and then bake for about 12–15 minutes, or until pale golden brown.

Allow to cool slightly on the baking sheets before transferring to a rack to cool completely. Store in an airtight container for up to a week.

easter biscuits

280 g (10 oz) plain white flour
2.5 ml (1 teaspoon) baking powder
140 g (5 oz) cold unsalted butter, cubed
140 g (5 oz) castor sugar
finely grated zest of 1 lemon
55 g (2 oz) currants
1 egg, beaten

makes
about 12 biscuits

My mum used to make these biscuits all year round, not just at Easter, when we were kids. They are simple and delicious.

Preheat the oven to 200°C/400°F/Gas Mark 6. Lightly grease a baking sheet.

Sift the flour and baking powder together into a bowl or process them together for a few seconds, to mix. Carefully rub the butter into the flour or add the butter to the processor bowl and pulse until the mixture looks like fine breadcrumbs. Transfer to a bowl if using a processor and then stir in the lemon zest, currants and egg. Mix well until it forms a dough.

Roll out on a lightly floured surface to about 5 mm (¼ inch) thick. Use an 8 cm (3½-inch) cutter to cut out the biscuits. Re-roll the trimmings to make more biscuits. Place on the baking sheet and bake for 10–12 minutes or until golden brown all over.

Remove from the oven and leave to cool slightly before removing to a wire rack to cool completely. Store in an airtight container for up to a week.

fruity flapjack-granola

175 g (6 oz) porridge oats

55 g (2 oz) raisins or currants

2 pinches of salt

55 g (2 oz) unrefined castor sugar

finely grated zest of 1 lemon,
plus juice of ½ a lemon

140 g (5 oz) unsalted butter, melted

55 g (2 oz) runny honey

30 ml (2 tablespoons) golden syrup

serves 6-8

One thing I really hate is a flapjack that is not moist; overcooked flapjacks are awful, too crunchy and jaw-breaking. This recipe is a cross between a flapjack and a granola, the breakfast cereal you get in America. It can be eaten on its own or broken up slightly and eaten with cold milk for breakfast.

Preheat the oven to 160°C/325°F/Gas Mark 3. Lightly oil a 22 cm (8¾-inch) square baking tin.

Mix together the oats, raisins or currants, salt, sugar and lemon zest. Add the butter, honey, golden syrup and lemon juice and mix well. Spoon into the baking tin and press down lightly and then bake for about 25–30 minutes, or until set and slightly browned around the outside. Allow to cool before breaking up into pieces.